Beyond the Letters

The Empty High After the MD, JD, or PhD—Tools to
Prevent Burnout, Recover Identity, and Redefine Success

Nicci Brochard
&
Dr. Ben Chuba

Beyond the Letters

The Empty High After the MD, JD, or PhD—Tools to
Prevent Burnout, Recover Identity, and Redefine Success

CROSSBORDER

New York, London, Quebec

Contents

Chapter 6: Reclaiming Identity – Rediscovering the Person Behind the Professional 85

Chapter 7: Success, Redefined – Crafting a Fulfilling Future on Your Terms 103

Epilogue...114

Introduction

The day the letters land after your name, you expect the world to tilt. Applause, a robe, a license on the wall—and then a hush you did not anticipate. The mountain has been climbed, the summit selfie taken, yet the view feels oddly flat. Colleagues call you doctor, counselor, professor. Inside, a quieter question stirs: who am I now?

Burnout often hides in prestige's shadow. The calendar overflows while the soul runs a deficit. Overtime becomes identity; perfection becomes oxygen. Many high achievers learn to outperform their doubts, but few learn to befriend themselves once the race slows. The result can be the empty high: a rush without meaning, a title without a tether.

For physicians, attorneys, and scholars, training prizes endurance and flawless output. The MD marches through call nights, the JD through billable hours, the PhD through publish-or-perish rituals. These rites forge competence and credibility, yet erode wonder, relationships, and health. Tradeoffs are named and healed.

This book offers a reset. Through field-tested tools, short reflections, and compact experiments, you will build a sturdier foundation: values that guide decisions, boundaries that protect attention, recovery rituals that restore energy, and conversations that reconnect you with purpose. Learn to audit commitments, design humane schedules, renegotiate expectations, and translate ambition into sustainable practice. Replace

1

performative productivity with genuine progress. Measure success by alignment, not applause.

Expect candor. Expect relief. Expect a return to the reasons that brought you here in the first place. Degrees can open doors, yet vocation flourishes when inner life and outer work move in step.

Step back from the ledge of constant proving. Step toward craft, contribution, and community. You earned the letters; now write a life that reads true. The empty high will not have the last word. A fuller chapter waits—clearer, kinder, and more alive.

Chapter 1

When the Applause Fades –
Confronting the Empty High

When the applause finally dies down and the dust of celebration settles, a curious silence often follows. Picture a newly minted Ph.D. alone in a quiet office the morning after the graduation gala, or a physician waking up the day after earning that coveted M.D., the congratulatory messages already slowing. The grand goal that fueled years of effort has been achieved – yet instead of permanent euphoria, there is a puzzling hollowness. That "empty high" can be as disorienting as it is unexpected. It turns out that reaching the summit of a long-sought achievement, whether academic or professional, often does not deliver endless joy. Psychologists describe this disillusionment as a kind of arrival fallacy – the false hope that *once* we make it to our destination, we'll be happy *forever*. In this chapter, we explore why that illusion is so compelling to high achievers, what emotional aftermath frequently ensues, how widespread this experience really is (hint: you're in good company), and how one confronts the *"What now?"* question that echoes in the quiet moments after the accolades. Grounded in real-world evidence and contemporary science, this discussion serves as both a practical guide and a philosophical reflection on finding purpose beyond the applause.

The Arrival Fallacy – Chasing Happiness in Achievements

For many strivers, it begins with a deeply ingrained story: *"Once I accomplish X, then I'll finally be truly happy."* This seductive idea is what Harvard-trained psychologist Tal Ben-Shahar famously termed the arrival fallacy, defined as the false belief that achieving a specific goal will bring a lasting, enduring happiness. High achievers in rigorous fields are especially prone to this mindset. It's easy to assume that earning the elite degree or landing the top job – reaching the M.D., J.D., or Ph.D. after years of sacrifice – will be the magic moment after which contentment is on cruise control. The reality, however, often tells a different story: the satisfaction of that achievement, while real, is fleeting.

Modern psychology and countless real-life experiences show that the burst of joy at reaching a goal is usually temporary. We adapt surprisingly fast to our accomplishments. In fact, there's a well-documented concept in behavioral science called the hedonic treadmill – no matter what high or low we experience, we tend to return to a personal baseline of happiness over time. We keep chasing the next milestone because each "arrival" fails to permanently boost our happiness; it's as if we're running in place emotionally. This is why the arrival fallacy is a *fallacy*: achieving that dream job, prestigious award, or any external milestone might give us a short-term high, but we soon discover life settling back into its usual rhythm. In one illustrative study, even people who won the lottery – a drastic positive life change – were not significantly happier than anyone else after the initial thrill, and they actually reported taking less pleasure in everyday activities than before. We often *think* the next achievement will finally secure bliss, but our brains just don't work that way in the long run.

Why do so many intelligent, driven individuals fall for this illusion? Part of the answer lies in cultural conditioning. From a young age, society teaches us that success *equals* happiness – get the degrees, the accolades, the income, and you've "made it." Children are often raised to believe that personal achievement is the key to a good life, sometimes more emphasized than qualities like empathy or balance. It's no wonder that by the time we're ambitious adults, we internalize a goal-oriented mindset that constantly looks to the *next* victory as the solution to any current discontent. Yet research consistently shows that external markers of success – money, titles, awards – do not bring lasting happiness. Psychologists have found that elements like meaningful relationships, engaging experiences, and one's outlook play a far greater role in long-term well-being than any trophy on the shelf. We *naively assume* that if our present efforts lead to triumph, we will automatically feel fulfilled in the future. If only it were that simple.

The truth dawning on many high achievers is that the next big achievement won't magically fix everything. Reaching a summit can be exhilarating, but it doesn't fundamentally change who you are or inoculate you against unhappiness. "I'll be happy when…" is a moving target – as soon as one goal is reached, the horizon shifts to another goal beyond. This constant horizon-chasing leaves little room to savor the present. One executive described it as climbing a ladder only to find it leaning on the wrong wall. The arrival fallacy sets us up to experience a peculiar disappointment: after the initial applause, we're left asking why permanent happiness hasn't arrived with our diploma or promotion in hand. In the next sections, we confront what that disappointment feels like and how common it really is.

The Empty Aftermath – When Success Feels Surprisingly Hollow

Shortly after a major goal is finally achieved, many high performers encounter what we can call the empty aftermath – a numb, ungrounded feeling that can follow in the wake of success. It's both paradoxical and jarring. You've done everything you set out to do, so shouldn't you feel on top of the world? Instead, you find yourself wrestling with a strange void. Psychologists describe this state in stark terms: *"Post-achievement depression involves experiencing a sense of purposelessness or sadness after completing a long-standing goal,"* accompanied by a complex mix of emotions. In this lull after the finish line, people report feeling fatigued, restless, deflated, or melancholic despite their success. There can be physical exhaustion, yes, but also a deeper spiritual fatigue – a feeling of *"Is that all there is?"* that can manifest as everything from mild blues to an existential crisis.

This phenomenon is so common among achievers that it has earned colloquial names. Some call it the "summit syndrome," referring to that *crash and burn* moment after you've reached your personal summit. You pour all your energy and identity into conquering a towering goal – be it launching a business, completing a marathon, or finishing your dissertation – only to find that upon reaching the top, there's a dizzying drop in purpose. As one observer put it, *you've lost the mission that got you out of bed every morning.* The big project that organized your life is over, and suddenly your calendar and your soul are wide open. This emptiness often feels disproportionate: you might think *"I should be thrilled, not listless!"* which can lead to guilt or confusion. But in truth, this letdown is an almost *natural neurochemical consequence* of achieving something grand.

Contemporary neuroscience sheds light on why the high doesn't last. Human brains are literally wired to derive satisfaction from pursuit and progress – the *chase* stimulates us as much as, if not more than, the finish. Neurobiologist Andrew Huberman and others have popularized how dopamine, the brain's motivation chemical, surges as we make strides toward a goal. Each small win along the journey fires up our reward circuitry, propelling us forward with excitement. However, when we finally *hit* the target, that steady dopamine propulsion can abruptly decline. In effect, the neurological engine that was driving us goes a bit quiet. The result? A short-lived burst of satisfaction followed by a sudden absence of that pursuing thrill – an emotional vacuum. It's the classic wisdom of "it's not the destination, it's the journey" now backed by biology. The journey kept you engaged and alive with purpose; the destination, once reached, removes that daily dose of drive, leaving you bereft of the thrill you had during the chase.

Beyond brain chemistry, there's also a psychological contrast effect at play. After a peak experience, the ordinary routines of life can feel *diminished.* Something as simple as returning to regular daily tasks or facing a free afternoon with no urgent goal can seem oddly colorless after the intense push toward achievement. Some new Ph.D. graduates half-joke that after defending their thesis, even checking email feels strange because there's no looming dissertation to procrastinate. Similarly, elite athletes often describe the days after a big competition as disturbingly quiet and directionless – the bigger the build-up, the more empty the aftermath can feel. The mind craves another mountain to climb, but immediately finding one isn't so simple, and in the interim a gloom can settle in.

Crucially, feeling this void does not mean something is wrong with you. It doesn't mean your accomplishment was pointless or that you're an ungrateful person. It means you're human, with a goal-driven mind that needs time to recalibrate. In fact, many achievers report a mix of restlessness and loss of identity in this phase. You might catch yourself asking, *"What do I do now, if I'm not the person working toward that goal? Who am I without this project occupying me?"* These questions can strike at the core of how we define ourselves. The next section will show that these unsettling feelings are far more common than most realize – a reassuring reminder that you are not alone in this experience.

Not Alone at the Top – A Common Letdown Shared by Many

Perhaps one of the most comforting truths about the post-achievement letdown is that it is surprisingly common across careers and endeavors. If you have felt a quiet disappointment after reaching a long-sought summit, you are in excellent company. In fact, psychologists note that this experience *"can happen in all walks of life"* – it's a shared human experience that resonates with people from diverse paths. New physicians finishing residency, attorneys passing the bar, academics securing their doctorate, writers completing a book, athletes winning championships – so many have privately felt that unsettling *"okay… now what?"* after the celebrations ended. The faces of success that we admire from afar often conceal this universal truth: even after standing at the pinnacle of achievement, many individuals grapple with an unexpected sense of isolation or letdown.

Real-world examples abound, cutting across the spectrum from ordinary people to the most famous. Consider the world of sports: Olympic athletes train for years with singular focus, yet it's well documented that post-Olympic depression strikes a vast number of them once the Games are over. The most decorated Olympian of all time, swimmer Michael Phelps, has candidly spoken about the profound emptiness he faced after accomplishing his life's goals. In his case, after winning multiple gold medals, he found himself atop the proverbial mountain asking, *"What the hell am I supposed to do?... Who am I?"*. This raw question from someone at the absolute peak of success illustrates that even achieving the highest honors can leave a person questioning their purpose. Phelps admitted that after the high of competition, he fell into a severe depression – a "crash" so intense that he contemplated whether he even wanted to be alive, until he sought help and a new way forward. His story is a powerful reminder: *you are not alone in feeling unfulfilled right after you achieve what you've always wanted.*

The phenomenon reaches beyond sports. Astronaut Buzz Aldrin, one of the first humans to walk on the Moon, experienced a famously difficult aftermath to that historic achievement. Upon returning to Earth after Apollo 11, Aldrin was greeted with ticker-tape parades and global acclaim – the ultimate *applause*. Yet inside, he felt deeply unsettled and purposeless. With poignant honesty, he wrote that after such a triumph, *"I wanted to resume my duties, but there were no duties to resume… There was no goal, no sense of calling, no project worth pouring myself into."*. Imagine that: a man who had literally achieved what millions dream of (travelling to the Moon) found himself drifting in a personal abyss afterward. Aldrin's depression and search for direction in the years following the Moon landing are well-chronicled, and they resonate with the same summit syndrome so many others quietly endure. If even a moonwalker can feel that *nothing will ever top this* desolation, it underscores that post-achievement emptiness does not discriminate by level of success.

Closer to home, countless lesser-known examples affirm the ubiquity of this pattern. New graduates often confess that in the weeks after finishing their degree, they felt oddly *down* or aimless despite their hard-won credentials. First-time authors sometimes report a "post-book blues" once the manuscript is sent off – suddenly, the imaginative fever of writing is gone, and everyday life feels anticlimactic. Startup founders who sell their company (netting a life-changing success) often struggle emotionally in the aftermath, missing the adrenaline of the startup grind. Even surgeons and other high-intensity professionals describe a similar dip in mood after completing an intense project or achieving a career milestone. The specifics differ, but the underlying sentiment is remarkably consistent: *reaching the top can feel surprisingly lonely.*

Knowing how common this is can be a source of solace and understanding. It's not a personal failing or a sign that you "don't appreciate your success enough." Rather, it's a nearly ubiquitous human response to the end of a challenging journey. One mental health writer observed that you aren't alone – it's common for people to feel depressed, disappointed, anxious, or empty after they've reached a goal. Simply realizing that many others – including those you admire – have walked this same road of post-achievement letdown can be validating. It means we can talk about it without shame. High achievers are often seen as invulnerable or perpetually confident, but in truth they may share this quiet doubt and disappointment. By shedding light on it, we take an important step toward moving through it. And that brings us to the pivotal turning point many face amid this void: the "What now?" moment.

The "What Now?" Moment – Finding Purpose Beyond the Applause

Sooner or later, the moment arrives when you're alone with your thoughts, the applause just a memory, and one question loud in your mind: *"What now?"* This "What now?" moment is a crossroads every achiever must navigate. It often strikes in a simple scene – for example, late at night after the party is over, you catch your own reflection in the dark window and feel the weight of silence. The goal that defined you for so long is behind you. The accolades have been collected, the congratulatory emails tapering off. Is this all there is? The frightening beauty of this moment is that it forces a confrontation with yourself, beyond any titles or awards.

Many high achievers initially experience this as a wave of anxiety or confusion. The psychiatrist who finally becomes an attending physician might sit at the desk on the first day of the new job feeling strangely unanchored without the next exam or qualification to strive for. The freshly minted Ph.D. wakes up asking, *"Who am I, if I'm not the stressed graduate student working toward a Ph.D.?"* It's a moment of reckoning, where you realize that achieving your goal answered the questions of *external* validation but unearthed more fundamental questions about identity and purpose. Michael Phelps described it vividly when he recounted how after his Olympic high, he stood wondering *"What the hell am I supposed to do?… Where am I supposed to go? Who am I?"* once the peak was behind him. That stark questioning captures the essence of the "What now?" crisis: you must figure out what fills your life with meaning when the applause has faded and the external impetus is gone.

Yet, within this daunting question lies an opportunity – the chance to redefine fulfillment on your own terms. Indeed, many achievers eventually come to see the "What now?" moment as a *turning point* rather than an ending. The key is to not run from that uncomfortable void, but to engage with it. Psychological guidance suggests a few steps here. First, simply *acknowledging* what you feel is crucial. Give yourself permission to feel a bit lost or disappointed without immediately judging it. As one expert advises, recognize and understand what you're experiencing, and even talk to others who have felt similarly – you'll likely discover that post-achievement malaise is prevalent and nothing to be ashamed of. Sharing these feelings with trusted peers or mentors can validate that it's normal, and their stories may shed light on a path forward.

Next comes reflection. It can be profoundly helpful to reflect on the journey that got you here. Ask yourself: *What was it about this goal or process that truly motivated me to begin with?* Did you love the *process* of getting there – the learning, the camaraderie, the challenge – or were you holding out for the end reward to make it all worthwhile? This reflection can illuminate a lot. As one psychologist put it, consider whether you found the process engaging, or if you were under the illusion that the result alone would justify all the hardship. If the process had meaning, those aspects can point you toward what to pursue next (perhaps it's the research itself, the creative act, the teamwork that you valued). If the process was miserable and only the end appealed to you, that's a signal too – maybe the goal wasn't aligned with your deeper passions, or you sacrificed more balance than was healthy. In either case, you gain insight into what truly matters to you, which is gold for rebuilding your sense of purpose.

Moving forward from "What now?" often involves shifting your focus from external validation to internal fulfillment. The end of one quest can be the start of a new kind of journey – one where the goals might be defined not by societal applause, but by personal meaning. For example, some newly graduated doctors, after grappling with post-achievement emptiness, decide to channel their energy into mastering the craft of medicine and finding daily purpose in patient care rather than in titles. A lawyer who hits the career milestone may start mentoring junior colleagues or engaging in community work to find renewed inspiration. Many high achievers turn to new challenges – sometimes wholly different in nature – to reignite their motivation. It's wise, however, to choose these new goals with the lesson of the arrival fallacy in mind: rather than chasing *another* shiny accolade, think about pursuits that are rewarding in and of themselves.

Research on happiness offers a guiding light here. Long-term studies have found that true and lasting fulfillment tends to come from fundamental things like *relationships, personal growth,* and *contribution,* more so than from fame or money. The Harvard Study of Adult Development (an 75-year longitudinal research) famously concluded that warm relationships are a stronger predictor of happiness than any professional success. In practical terms, this means that reconnecting with family and friends, or fostering new supportive relationships, might do more for your well-being than diving immediately into the next work project. It suggests that the "new purpose" you seek could be oriented around community, creativity, or caring – values that endure beyond any single achievement. Many accomplished people eventually discover that mentoring others, for instance, brings a satisfaction that surpasses the thrill of their own past achievements. Likewise, pursuing hobbies, health, or neglected interests can reintroduce joy and meaning that isn't tied to one's resume. These are not idle platitudes, but evidence-backed insights: focusing on simple sources of happiness and on connections with others is proven to guard against the depression and stress that can follow intense goal pursuit.

Of course, finding a new equilibrium doesn't happen overnight. There may be a period of discomfort as you transition from the old goal to new horizons. It's important in this time to take care of your mental health. Some individuals benefit from professional support, such as therapy or coaching, to navigate the identity shift – as Michael Phelps did when he sought therapy and learned to manage his depression and anxiety in the years after his Olympic triumphs. Others simply need a break – a chance to rest, recharge, and let new inspirations emerge naturally. One common piece of advice is not to make impulsive life changes in the immediate aftermath of an achievement just to fill the void; instead, allow yourself to sit with the feelings for a while. As one writer noted, after the drive vanishes it's perfectly natural for it to leave a void – you can accept that as part of the cycle, take time to recharge, and then step into your next phase a little wiser.

Consider the story of Buzz Aldrin once more. His "What now?" moment was earth-shaking – he literally had to come back *down to Earth* after walking on the Moon. He struggled for a time, turning to unhealthy coping mechanisms as he felt aimless. But eventually, Aldrin confronted his feelings and sought a new purpose. He underwent treatment for depression, fought his way through alcoholism, and gradually reshaped his life's mission. In the years after his darkest period, he found meaning in advocating for mental health, authoring books, and contributing to space education. He transformed his legacy from just *astronaut* to also *mentor, author,* and *mental health advocate.* In doing so, he proved that even the steepest post-achievement abyss can be climbed out of, one step at a time, by forging new purpose beyond the original accolade.

When the applause fades, it may reveal an unexpected quiet – but in that quiet is a chance to hear the inner voice of what you truly want next. The end of one journey is not the end of your story. It can be the beginning of a deeper quest for meaning that transcends trophies and titles. By understanding the arrival fallacy, you guard against the false promise that *another* achievement is the cure. By recognizing the empty aftermath for what it is – a temporary void, even a natural comedown – you can approach it with patience and self-compassion rather than panic. By knowing you're not alone, you tap into the wisdom and support of a community of achievers who have been there too. And by bravely asking "What now?" you open the door to growth. The answer to that question may lead you to redefine success in richer, more fulfilling terms: not as a finish line, but as an ongoing journey of purpose. In the chapters to come, we will continue to build on this foundation, exploring how to find enduring motivation, balance ambition with well-being, and ensure that the next peaks you climb are aligned with a truly satisfying life beyond the applause.

Chapter 2

Burning Bright, Burning Out – The High Cost of High Achievement

High achievers – whether they are physicians, attorneys, professors, or creative professionals – often burn bright in their fields. Their dedication, drive, and talent shine intensely. But that intense flame can come at a high cost. This chapter explores how relentless pursuit of excellence can slip into exhaustion and burnout. Grounded in scientific research and real-world stories, we illuminate the hidden struggles behind outward success. The tone here is both informational and inspirational: understanding the problem is the first step toward overcoming it.

Candle at Both Ends

One common trait of top performers is an almost superhuman work ethic. Burning the candle at both ends becomes routine. A surgeon arrives at the hospital before dawn, finishes after dark, then pores over charts late into the night. A trial lawyer stays past midnight preparing for a case, fueled by coffee and a fear of falling short. An academic spends weekends in the lab or grading papers, driven by *"publish or perish"* pressure. These relentless schedules can push even the most energetic individuals toward exhaustion. In one illustrative case, a dedicated primary care physician in Boston tried working "part-time" – yet her *part-time* role demanded well over 40 hours a week. She would leave home at

5:30 AM to beat traffic and return home drained: "I was exhausted," she admits. Long days blurred into long nights, and even a reduced schedule felt unsustainable. Her experience echoes a familiar pattern among high achievers across fields: long hours and little downtime become the norm, not the exception.

Why do accomplished professionals drive themselves so hard? Often, it's due to a combination of external demands and self-imposed pressure. Many elite professionals are, by nature, perfectionists and overachievers. This trait can be a double-edged sword. On one hand, perfectionism fuels high-quality work; on the other, it sets an impossible standard and an incessant internal voice saying *"not enough."* One physician described this mindset candidly: *"Being a typical physician perfectionist and overachiever, I wanted my [organization] to perform well, and I felt singularly responsible for our success."*. In other words, he put the weight of the world on his own shoulders. Many doctors, lawyers, and academics do the same – they feel personally responsible for every outcome, every patient or client, every student or project. This weight of responsibility can become crushing over time.

Several structural factors in high-achievement careers also encourage burning the candle at both ends. In medicine, 12-hour shifts or 36-hour on-call duties have long been an accepted reality. In the legal profession, excessive hours are practically a badge of honor – one report found 86% of lawyers regularly work outside the standard 9-to-5 workday, and 73% routinely work on weekends. Academia is no less demanding: faculty often juggle teaching, research, and administrative tasks that spill well beyond a 40-hour week, with one study finding professors working 60+

hours on average. Creative industries and tech start-ups likewise propagate a 24/7 hustle culture. The message is clear: *always be working*. High achievers internalize this message, often to their detriment.

Over time, running at full throttle with minimal rest takes a physiological and mental toll. The human body and mind cannot operate at peak intensity indefinitely without recovery. Yet many ambitious professionals ignore this reality. They skip lunch to squeeze in more work, sacrifice sleep to refine a project, and forsake vacations due to a sense of indispensability. In the moment, it might feel necessary or even exhilarating – the thrill of productivity and achievement. But as the weeks and months pile up, fatigue accumulates. What starts as a bright flame of passion can falter and start to burn out if it's not carefully managed. Burning the candle at both ends, unfortunately, often leads to burning out the candle entirely.

Cracks in the Façade

On the outside, our high achievers still *look* successful. The doctor dons a confident smile for patients; the lawyer delivers polished arguments in court; the professor lectures energetically to a hall of students. All seems well from the exterior. But behind this polished façade, cracks may be forming. The term "burnout" in psychology describes exactly these cracks – the internal erosion of energy and engagement that can lurk behind a successful exterior. Burnout has been defined as a state of chronic workplace stress characterized by three key dimensions: overwhelming exhaustion, cynicism or detachment, and a sense of inefficacy or lack of accomplishment. In simpler terms, a burned-out high performer feels emotionally drained, becomes increasingly cynical (or indifferent) about their work and the people they serve, and experiences a diminished sense of achievement. They may even start to question their identity in their role.

Consider the *classic signs of burnout* that might hide behind a "perfect" professional's smile:

- **Emotional exhaustion:** A profound fatigue that isn't cured by a good night's sleep. The person feels **worn out** and depleted every day. For example, an attorney described reaching a point where *"the stress level got so high that I didn't want to get up in the morning and go to work"*, even though she once loved her job. This level of exhaustion goes beyond ordinary tiredness – it's a bone-deep weariness that saps the joy out of work and life.

- **Cynicism and detachment:** A growing sense of negativity, cynicism, or alienation from one's work. The compassionate doctor finds herself becoming curt with patients, or feeling emotionally numb in situations that once moved her. The dedicated teacher starts referring to students as "numbers" or "problems" rather than individuals. This is sometimes called depersonalization – a protective emotional distancing. One physician admitted that under relentless stress *"I became progressively detached and short-tempered"*. Likewise, a burned-out lawyer might feel a wave of dread on Monday mornings and think, *"I can't pretend to care about these cases anymore."* That loss of connection and empathy is a telltale crack in the façade.

- **Reduced sense of accomplishment:** Even though the individual might still be high-performing by external standards, inside they feel ineffective and unsuccessful. They have trouble finding pride or meaning in their work. Achievements that used to be fulfilling now feel hollow. An accomplished academic might win a grant or publish a paper yet feel like a fraud, or think "it's not enough; I'm not good enough." This diminished personal accomplishment often comes with a loss of identity – since so many high achievers *are* their work, feeling unaccomplished strikes at the core of who they are. They wonder, *"If I'm not the brilliant doctor/lawyer/professor I set out to be, then who am I?"*

These cracks in the façade can be surprisingly well-hidden, especially by people who have always excelled. High achievers are often skilled at maintaining appearances of competence and composure. Colleagues, friends, even family might not realize anything is wrong, because outwardly the person is "holding it together." Indeed, the individual themselves may not initially recognize their state as burnout – they might dismiss it as simply stress or the price of success. They keep pushing forward, telling themselves to "tough it out," which unfortunately can deepen the cracks.

It's important to stress that burnout is not a sign of personal weakness or failure. Feeling these symptoms does not mean the doctor isn't cut out for medicine or the attorney can't hack it in law. On the contrary, burnout often strikes the most dedicated and conscientious individuals – the very people who *care* the most about doing a good job.

The *smiling perfectionist* may be silently crumbling inside, not because they don't belong in their career, but because they've been running at an unsustainable pace under intense pressure. Recognizing these signs for what they are – and not hiding or ignoring them – is crucial. Many professionals, unfortunately, ignore the early warning signs (irritability, fatigue, disillusionment) until they amplify into a full-blown crisis. We will next look at how widespread this problem really is – and the answer is eye-opening.

By the Numbers: A Crisis

If burnout lurked only in a few rare cases, one might write it off as an individual issue. But research shows that it has become a widespread crisis across high-achievement professions. Burnout is no longer just a personal concern; it's a systemic problem recognized by global health experts. In fact, the World Health Organization now classifies burnout as an "occupational phenomenon" resulting from chronic workplace stress. In other words, this is not about a few people not being "tough enough" – it's about work conditions and cultures that are driving people to a breaking point. The hard evidence is stark:

- **Physicians:** Nearly half of doctors in the United States report at least one symptom of burnout. A major 2024 study of thousands of U.S. physicians found 45.2% had at least one manifestation of burnout. During the worst of the COVID-19 pandemic, the rates were even higher – in 2021, 62.8% of physicians surveyed had one or more burnout symptoms. In other words, *more than every other doctor* you meet may be struggling with exhaustion or cynicism behind the scenes. This is truly epidemic levels among healers who are often seen as invincible.

- **Lawyers:** Similar burnout rates plague the legal profession. In late 2021, a Bloomberg Law survey found that attorneys reported being burned out more than half the time on the job. Another state-wide survey in 2022 showed over 75% of lawyers self-reported experiencing burnout, and nearly half had seriously considered leaving their job or even the profession as a result. Think about that – almost one in two lawyers has thought about quitting law because of stress and burnout. This isn't a few isolated "unhappy lawyers"; it's a reflection of deep, widespread fatigue in the legal field.

- **Academics:** Professors and academic staff are facing a burnout crisis as well. University faculty surveys indicate that roughly 6 in 10 faculty have felt burned out by their work. One report put the figure at 64% of faculty experiencing work-related burnout. The pressures of teaching (often large classes or heavy course loads), conducting research, securing grants, and serving on committees – all while often being underpaid or on precarious contracts – contribute to this high burnout rate. Academia, often idealized as an ivory tower, is for many a gauntlet of long hours and chronic stress, leading to profound exhaustion.

- **Other Creative/High-achievement Fields:** Although hard data can be scarcer, anecdotal evidence abounds that professionals in creative industries (writers, artists, designers) and tech entrepreneurs also suffer high burnout. The expectation to be constantly innovating and producing – to churn out the next novel, the next design, the next startup – can mirror the relentless pace of doctors or lawyers. The phenomenon is so common that phrases like "startup burnout" or "creative burnout" have entered our vocabulary. For instance, surveys of the broader workforce show record-high stress levels in recent years, with one 2022 report finding 79% of employees experienced work-related stress and nearly half felt physically or emotionally exhausted from their jobs. High-achievers are certainly not exempt from those trends; if anything, they may be *more* prone due to their workload and personal investment in their work.

All these numbers point to a sobering truth: burnout is pervasive and rising. It is not a personal failing of a few individuals who "couldn't handle the pressure." When roughly half or more of the members of any esteemed profession are reporting burnout symptoms, it signals a cultural and organizational crisis. Medicine, law, academia – these institutions have historically rewarded self-sacrifice and stamina. Now we see the consequences of that culture: brilliant people burning out in large numbers. Professional societies and even governments have begun to take note. The U.S. Surgeon General issued an advisory in 2022 warning that health worker burnout was leading to staffing shortages and threatening the healthcare system. The American Bar Association and academic leadership forums are likewise sounding alarms about mental health in their fields. Burnout has been identified as a serious threat not only to personal well-being but also to professional effectiveness, as a fatigued, cynical doctor or lawyer cannot serve others as safely or effectively. In sum, the data confirm what many have long suspected: we are dealing with an epidemic of chronic stress and fatigue among high achievers. The next question is, what happens if this burnout remains unaddressed?

Burnout's Fallout

The fallout from unaddressed burnout can be devastating – both for the individual and for the profession they belong to. At an individual level, chronic workplace stress left to fester can trigger a cascade of mental and physical health problems. Burnout isn't just "in your head"; it wreaks havoc on the body as well. Research has linked persistent job burnout to increased risk of serious health issues – including coronary heart disease, high cholesterol, Type 2 diabetes, insomnia, and clinical depression. Basically, years of unrelenting stress can age and strain the body's systems. Doctors often counsel patients about stress management to prevent heart attacks or strokes; ironically, the doctors themselves (and similarly stressed professionals) are at heightened risk when they ignore their own stress. Burnout also correlates with unhealthy coping behaviors – some people turn to alcohol or stimulants to prop themselves up, or overeat, or stop exercising, which only exacerbates the health toll. It's a vicious cycle: stress leads to poor health and poor habits, which lead to worse health and less energy, which makes work even harder.

Mentally and emotionally, burnout can slide into anxiety, depression, or despair. The emotional exhaustion and cynicism, if not checked, may evolve into a clinical depression or an anxiety disorder. It's telling (and tragic) that lawyers, for example, have one of the highest rates of depression and substance abuse among professions. In extreme cases, burnout can even contribute to suicidal thoughts. We should note that *suicide rates* have been higher than average in some high-stress professions (physicians and lawyers both have had concerning statistics in this regard), highlighting that burnout's ultimate fallout can be loss of life. While not everyone reaches that extreme, *hitting rock bottom* is a story shared surprisingly often by overachievers who burned out.

One common burnout rock-bottom narrative is the career collapse or exit. These are the doctors, lawyers, professors, etc., who abruptly quit or slowly drift out of the careers they once fought so hard to enter. Imagine spending a decade or more training and sacrificing to achieve a dream – and then walking away from it because it's destroying you. It's happening in significant numbers. *"Some of the best have headed for the exits,"* observed one physician who now counsels fellow doctors on burnout. In medicine, this trend is quantifiable: a 2023 study reported that roughly one-third of physicians were considering leaving their current practice (or reducing clinical hours significantly), with burnout and lack of fulfillment cited as key motivators. In the early 2020s, approximately 6% of U.S. physicians *actually left* medicine in a single year – that's tens of thousands of doctors dropping out, an alarming brain drain in healthcare. Law firms and academia see parallel trends: young lawyers opting out of big-law partnerships to preserve their sanity, professors taking early retirement or switching to less pressured roles because they can't endure the strain.

These departures often come after an intense period of inner turmoil. Consider an example of a mid-career physician – we'll call her *Dr. A*. She was the model of a caring doctor, beloved by patients and respected by colleagues. But quietly, Dr. A was deteriorating. Her part-time clinical job (as we saw earlier) had inexorably expanded to full-time-plus hours, and bureaucratic hassles (insurance coding, electronic record systems) eroded her joy in patient care. She recalls coming home numb: *"I was like a shell at home, because I was keeping it all together at work."*. This stark description shows how completely burnout can drain one's personal life – she had nothing left for her own family after expending all energy just to function at work. Eventually, in 2018, she stepped away from clinical medicine altogether. Almost immediately, she felt the difference: her family noticed she became *"a nicer person"* again, and her own sense of self began to repair. She started a small business on her own terms and rediscovered a sustainable sense of purpose. Now, Dr. A also hears from countless physicians nationwide who tell her they want out too, saying *"it is really, really, really a lot of people"* reaching a breaking point.

The story of Dr. A (and others like her) illustrates both the heavy toll of burnout and a glimmer of hope. Her life indeed hit a form of rock bottom – she left a career she once loved because it became untenable. But hitting that bottom also forced a moment of truth: *Why am I doing this? What else could I do?* In her case, acknowledging the severity of her burnout was the first step to reclaiming her life. She carved a new path and actually found happiness on the other side. Not everyone will or should leave their profession, of course. But even those who stay can attest that confronting burnout is transformative. One seasoned family doctor who came back from the brink of burnout reflected that the experience, painful as it was, ultimately made him a *"better doctor and a healthier person."*. He learned to set boundaries and refocus on what mattered in his work, and he sought therapy for support. Many others, once they face the issue head-on, discover similar insights and changes that allow them to continue in their fields with a new, healthier approach.

From a broader perspective, the fallout of burnout also hits organizations and society. When talented professionals leave en masse or become chronically disengaged, service quality suffers. For example, if half the professors at a university are burned out, students receive poorer mentorship and education. If experienced lawyers drop out, clients lose trusted advocates. If doctors cut their clinic hours, patients face longer waits and less continuity of care. A vicious cycle can ensue: the fewer professionals remaining, the more workload and stress on those left behind, which in turn breeds more burnout. This spiral can devastate entire departments or industries if not checked. That's why acknowledging and addressing burnout isn't just touchy-feely talk – it's critical for maintaining excellence in any high-stakes field.

Acknowledging burnout is the first step toward recovery. This cannot be overstated. A burned-out achiever often attempts to deny the problem – "I just need to work harder," "everyone else is managing, so I should too," or "it's just a phase." But denial only deepens the damage. Experts warn that the worst thing one can do is try to "tough it out" indefinitely. As one psychologist noted, many people feel invincible and just push themselves more, but that approach is counterproductive and dangerous.

Instead, it takes courage to pause and say, "I'm not okay." Admitting exhaustion or distress isn't a defeat for a high achiever – it's a brave and necessary act of self-preservation. It opens the door to getting help, whether that means talking to a mental health professional, confiding in trusted colleagues, or making changes in workload or career path. *"The first thing you have to do is stop and really pull back and find ways to self-care,"* advises Dr. Tené Lewis, an epidemiologist who studies stress. That might mean taking a real vacation, setting firmer work-hour limits, practicing mindfulness or exercise, or seeking organizational changes.

The inspirational insight here is that burnout is not a one-way street. Many who have hit bottom with burnout have managed to climb back up. They often emerge with a renewed sense of balance and a clearer idea of what they need (and do not need) in their work lives. Burnout, in hindsight, can act as a severe wake-up call – a signal that something must change. As painful as the experience is, it can lead to personal growth, healthier habits, or advocacy for better conditions in one's profession. For instance, physicians who survived burnout have gone on to champion wellness programs for healthcare workers. Lawyers who faced burnout now speak openly about mental health in the legal industry, eroding stigma. Academics have begun pushing universities to pay more attention to faculty well-being. In these ways, acknowledging burnout is not only the first step in an individual's recovery, but also the first step in changing the culture that caused it.

In conclusion, "Burning Bright, Burning Out" captures a poignant paradox: the same passion and commitment that drive people to greatness can, if unchecked, drive them into the ground. We have examined how the candle of high achievement, when burned at both ends, can gutter out into exhaustion. We have peeked behind the smiling façade to recognize the signs of burnout that many prefer to hide. We've seen through statistics that this is a widespread crisis, not a personal flaw. And we've confronted the fallout – the very real health risks, the career breakpoints, and the human costs of burnout. Yet within this tough reality lies hope and motivation. Burnout, once acknowledged, can be addressed. The flame that dimmed can be rekindled, this time in a more sustainable way. The first step is simply to shine light on the problem – to name it and face it. In doing so, the accomplished doctor, lawyer, scholar or creator is not showing weakness, but profound strength. It's a statement that my well-being matters, that one's brilliant career should not come at the expense of one's soul or sanity. Only by confronting the high cost of high achievement can we begin to reclaim a healthier, more fulfilling path forward, where bright minds continue to shine without burning out.

Chapter 3
The Vanishing Self – When Identity Gets Lost in a Title

Every day, high achievers pour heart and soul into becoming top professionals. They spend years in grueling training, collecting degrees and accolades, until a title like "Doctor," "Professor," "Attorney," or "Engineer" starts to feel less like a job and more like *who they are*. This chapter explores how an all-consuming career can meld with one's identity – and what happens when that defining role fades. We will see how elite training and praise can make a title synonymous with self, how people can feel aimless and "lost at sea" when the role ends, and how an unsettling crisis of purpose can emerge when one asks, "Who am I without this?" Finally, we'll look beyond the letters after our names to rediscover the person we always were, beneath the titles.

Defined by the Title

Years of Investment in a Role: Ambitious professionals often dedicate their youth and energy to a single pursuit, whether medicine, academia, law, technology, or another field. After so much effort, the *title* they earn becomes a shorthand for their entire identity. A physician who has trained for a decade may admit, "we have labored so long to achieve the right to call ourselves 'doctor' that it has become part of our identity". The letters M.D. or Ph.D. or J.D. come to feel inseparable from the person. Friends, family, and colleagues reinforce this by using the title as a name – *the* Doctor, *the* Professor – signaling respect but also unintentionally equating the individual with their role. Psychologists note that we often answer the question "What do you do?" with "I *am* a [job title]," using a "to be" verb that binds our occupation to our sense of self. For example, law students quickly learn to say "I am a lawyer" rather than "I practice law," and in doing so they internalize that their profession *is* their identity. In the tech world, a software engineer might be dubbed "the coding genius," or a startup founder might be seen by peers *only* as "the CEO."

Persona and Prestige: The phenomenon isn't just linguistic – it's deeply psychological. Over time, the prestige and routine of the career create a professional persona that can dominate one's whole self-concept. The famed psychoanalyst Carl Jung observed that each profession comes with a ready-made persona, and people can become *identical* with that persona: *"the professor with his textbook, the tenor with his voice"*. At first, being fully "Doctor" or "Professor" can feel positive – it's a badge of honor reflecting hard-earned expertise. Medical culture, for instance, often expects doctors to live and breathe medicine. As one commenter noted, "the all-consuming work required to achieve [the goal of becoming a physician]... has something to do with [losing your identity in your profession]". Academia, too, encourages total immersion. Many graduate students spend the entirety of their formative adult years in school, moving from college to master's to PhD without a break. One newly minted Ph.D. described that by age 29, she had been in school continuously for 25 years and had *"few memories of [herself] before school"*.

Being a student and then a scholar became "a convenient explanation and stand-in for who you are" after so long. In other words, the role subsumed the individual.

Hard to Separate Person from Credentials: When professional success arrives, society applauds – and sometimes only sees – the title. A surgeon might notice how proud their family looks when introducing them as *a doctor*, or a professor hears even friends preface their name with "Professor" as if it were a part of their identity. This recognition is gratifying, but it blurs the line between *what you do* and *who you are*. With the validation and self-worth tied so tightly to the role, it becomes difficult to peel the credentials away from the person behind them. In the legal field, for example, young attorneys are taught that being a lawyer means doing certain tasks; if they aren't drafting briefs or arguing in court, they feel they "aren't lawyers" at all. This task-oriented identity means any deviation from the role can shake their self-image. Similarly in tech, the entrepreneurial mindset often glorifies total dedication – founders who eat, sleep, and breathe their startup. It's not unusual to see an "entrepreneurial identity" engulf one's lifestyle, to the point that *everything* – where one lives, who one socializes with, how one dresses – revolves around being a startup founder. Whether it's the white coat, the academic regalia, the courtroom suit, or the Silicon Valley hoodie, the uniform and title can fuse with the person. Over time, the title-carrier might wonder if anything is left of *them* apart from their work. After striving so long to finally become "the Doctor," "the Professor," or "the CEO," the individual may inadvertently allow the title to define their entire identity.

Yet as natural as it is to take pride in a hard-won title, there is a quiet danger in letting it wholly define us. If identity becomes one-dimensional – *only* the role – what happens when that role changes or ends? The next sections explore how life can feel unmoored when the title that once anchored one's identity is suddenly lost or left behind.

Lost at Sea

When the Structure Disappears: For many high achievers, day-to-day life during their climb is tightly structured. The medical resident has a regimented schedule; the PhD candidate knows exactly what experiments or papers to tackle; the lawyer working 60-hour weeks in a firm has every hour accounted for. The environment provides goals, feedback, and a sense of progress. But when that structured program or job ends – often quite abruptly – the sudden void can be jarring. One newly minted Ph.D. vividly described how upon finishing her program, *"having it suddenly end [left her] feeling lost at sea"*. During grad school she had worked 70+ hours a week with a clear purpose; afterward, she woke up with no classes, no research deadlines, no built-in routine. She found herself wandering aimlessly – even doing something as mundane as *"brows[ing] the cereal aisle at 11 pm on a Tuesday"* because she didn't know what else to do. Such aimlessness was completely foreign to her after years of being driven by academic goals.

This sense of being adrift without a compass can strike anyone whose defining structure is removed. A brand new physician who finally finishes training might unexpectedly miss the dictated schedule of residency once the supportive environment of supervisors and co-residents is gone. A tech professional who poured their identity into a startup can feel strangely idle and directionless if the company shuts down or they step away. Even a top student who graduates into a gap period can feel a bewildering emptiness where their school routine used to be. The feeling is often described in metaphors of being adrift: *rudderless, anchorless,* or as that PhD put it, *"lost at sea."* Without the title or institution telling you where to be and what to strive for, days that were once overflowing with purpose can start to feel painfully empty.

Aimlessness and Emotional Drift: The emotional impact of this aimlessness can be significant. Without a clear role, people often lose their sense of direction and self-worth. Mental health experts note that the *"loss of identity, routine, and goals can impact your sense of self-worth, leave you feeling rudderless, or even lead to depression."* When someone who has been known as "the Doctor" or "the Professor" steps away from that role, they may wake up asking, *"What is my worth today?"* without patients or students depending on them. For example, newly retired professionals frequently struggle with this adjustment. If you're no longer a doctor, a teacher, a programmer, or a pilot – *who are you?* It's common for retirees to face exactly that question: *"If you're no longer a [your job], who are you?".* Often, they also miss the social interaction and sense of importance that came with the job. Similarly, a lawyer who leaves a prestigious firm might feel invisible without the status and the packed calendar. One day you have a team calling you for decisions; the next day, your phone is silent.

Real-world stories illustrate how quickly a sense of self can drift. A freshly graduated attorney who doesn't land the expected big-firm job can feel unmoored, no longer the star student or "future lawyer" that defined them throughout school. In the tech industry, there are founders who sell their startup or shut it down and then wake up the next morning with no code to write, no team meetings – and they describe an almost existential drift. All the momentum suddenly stops. One tech founder wrote of the moment after stepping down: "I had nowhere I had to be and no one needing me. I felt like I was floating, unsure which direction land was" (as one might describe being lost at sea).

Narrative Example – The New PhD: Let's return to the PhD who felt "lost at sea," as her story paints the picture in human terms. After the intense final push to complete her doctorate, she expected to feel elated. Instead, when the congratulations messages died down, she found herself sinking into listlessness. *"Without grad school, I have been aimless,"* she admitted, describing not just the practical uncertainty of *"what am I going to do next,"* but a deeper malaise. She would cry over tiny things and felt frightened each morning at the prospect of a day with no structure. Hobbies that she once enjoyed had lost their appeal, and even basic self-care was disrupted (she lost access to her student health insurance and could not afford therapy in this vulnerable period). People around her kept asking how she was celebrating her big achievement, but she felt guilty that she *didn't* feel like celebrating. In her words, *"I am proud of my Ph.D. I am not proud of what I allowed myself to go through to earn this degree."* The structure that had sustained her was gone, and with it went her sense of direction. Her experience, while sobering, is not unique. Many graduates, ex-military personnel, or employees leaving an all-consuming job report a similar period of drift. The external framework that guided their days vanishes, and until they find a new course, they feel stranded in a vast open sea of possibilities – which can be more paralyzing than freeing at first.

The phrase "lost at sea" captures both the fear and confusion of this state. There is an ocean of time and options, but no familiar stars or compass to navigate by. It's a dangerous phase where some people flounder or sink into depression. However, it is also a transitional phase – one that, with support and reflection, can eventually lead to a new course. First, though, comes an even more profound challenge: confronting the void of purpose that the lost title leaves behind.

Crisis of Purpose

"Who Am I Without This?" This haunting question lies at the heart of the crisis faced by those whose identity was anchored to a title. When a defining chapter ends – graduation, retirement, a career change, or even achieving a long-sought goal – high achievers can be struck by an unsettling emptiness. Having spent years being *the* doctor, *the* professor, *the* star, they now look in the mirror and aren't sure who they see. One academic, reflecting on her post-PhD depression, put it plainly: it wasn't the tough job market or stress per se that brought her down, but something deeper – *"a crisis of purpose, particularly the sense of loss that accompanies the end of a time of accomplishment and security."* During the program, her purpose had been clear: to learn, to contribute research, to earn that degree. Once it was over, that guiding purpose vanished, leaving a void. Humans have a fundamental *"desire for purpose,"* as she noted, and our purpose often shapes "who we are and how we are seen". So when the purpose is suddenly gone, it can feel like losing a piece of oneself.

This crisis of purpose doesn't only happen in academia. Consider a seasoned physician who has to stop practicing due to an injury or burnout – if healing others was their life's purpose, they will inevitably grapple with *"Who am I, if not a healer?"* Or a corporate executive who steps down after decades at the helm might ask, *"What is the point of my days now, without the meetings and decisions that used to fill them?"* In extreme cases, the loss of one's professional identity can be devastating to mental health. When a person's entire self-image is wrapped up in the job, removing the job can precipitate a true identity crisis. Career experts describe how *"role engulfment"* (when a single role consumes your identity) sets the stage for such a collapse – if that role ends, the person feels they've lost their very self. It's like a stool where all the legs but one have been removed. As one commentary noted, *"the loss of work… can provoke a severe identity crisis, with people asking: 'Who am I? What am I if I don't work?'"*. Those questions, once philosophical, become painfully real in the aftermath of a lost title.

Existential Void After a Pinnacle: Paradoxically, a crisis of purpose can hit even at what outwardly looks like a peak of success. Finishing a pinnacle achievement – be it defending a dissertation, making partner at a firm, selling a company, or winning an Olympic medal – can trigger a dark and unexpected slump. After the celebrations and congratulations, the achiever is left thinking, "It's over… now what?" The existential void opens up when one realizes that the big goal that sustained them for so long has been met (or the long road toward it has ended), and they have not defined a new purpose to replace it. Psychologists have observed this pattern in many fields. For example, elite athletes sometimes experience "post-Olympic blues" for this very reason: a life-defining purpose has been fulfilled, and in its wake comes a sense of drift or meaninglessness. In academia, the term "post-dissertation depression" is informally used to describe new PhDs' slump after the high of completion. As one PhD admitted, *"it is like finishing a marathon… only to realize you've agreed to compete in a triathlon every day for the rest of your career"* – a humorous exaggeration that nonetheless captures the fatigue and *"now what?"* feeling at the end of a long race. High achievers often climb and climb, expecting the summit to feel satisfying, but upon reaching it they sometimes find an unsettling silence.

For those whose career chapter is ending not by choice but by circumstance – say, a job loss, a failed venture, or mandatory retirement – the crisis can be sharpened by feelings of grief or failure. They not only ask *"Who am I without this?"* but also wrestle with *"Why did I lose this?"* Self-doubt and loss of meaning can feed each other in a vicious cycle. Steve's Story from earlier is a cautionary example: Steve was a medical student whose dream of becoming a physician was cut short when he had to leave school. In a single day he went from seeing himself as a future doctor to feeling like a nobody. He *"lost his identity the day he found out medical school was over"*, and the effect was catastrophic. Steve fell into a deep depression; his marriage fell apart, and he became suicidal – to the point that his distraught mother feared he would take his own life. His entire sense of purpose had revolved around that title "doctor," and when it vanished, so did his reason for being. Steve eventually recovered, but not everyone in his shoes does. Tragically, there are documented cases of professionals who never find a new purpose and succumb to despair. Physicians, for instance, have higher-than-average suicide rates, and loss of identity or purpose is often a contributing factor in those extreme outcomes.

Grappling With the Questions: The crisis of purpose forces people to confront hard questions about self-worth and meaning. In this void, some people feel *guilt* or *shame* – "I should be happy or productive, but I'm not." Others feel *fear*: if my purpose was tied to being a successful professional and I'm no longer in that role, does my life have less value now? It can truly feel like an *"existential void,"* as if one's very existence needs to be re-justified. During this time, individuals might withdraw or isolate, unsure how to present themselves to the world without their former status. Picture the professor whose introduction at parties used to spark admiration ("Oh, you're a professor of physics, how interesting!"); after retirement, he may dread the innocuous question "So, what do you do?" because he's no longer sure how to answer.

Importantly, this crisis, painful as it is, also presents an *opportunity*. As the academic blogger noted, the solution isn't necessarily to frantically find a *new* grand purpose right away. Rather, it may be to examine why one's entire sense of purpose was tethered to that title. In other words, why did being in academia (or medicine, law, etc.) become the sole source of meaning? Answering that can reveal a lot about one's values and needs. It can also open the possibility that meaning can come from other areas of life, which sets the stage for rebuilding a more balanced identity. The crisis of purpose is a stark reminder that a career, no matter how distinguished, is *one* chapter in a life, not the whole story. The next section will explore how to rediscover the rest of that story – the person behind the accolades – and how to reclaim a sense of self that isn't limited to a business card or diploma.

Beyond the Letters

The Person Behind the Professional: When a title has dominated our identity for so long, it's easy to forget that we are more than that title. But we are. You *existed* before you earned those credentials, and you continue to exist outside of them. The task now is to reconnect with that fuller self – the one that contains all the passions, values, quirks, and roles that make you *you*. As one physician-writer wisely noted, *"We would not cease to exist if [our] title went away. Being a [professional] should not define us."* In practical terms, this means actively separating your self-worth from your job title. It's a process of gentle untangling: recognizing that *what you do* is just one part of *who you are*. A lawyer-turned-career-coach put it this way: your job is about what you do, *"not who you are."* If you base your entire identity on being a lawyer (or doctor, professor, etc.), *"you set yourself up for an identity crisis"* when change inevitably comes. The alternative is to ground your identity in more enduring traits – your values, your character, your talents, and the relationships you cultivate – rather than in a title that can come and go.

So, who is the person behind the letters? It might help to literally list out aspects of yourself beyond work: Are you a parent? A friend? An artist, a traveler, a community member, a person of faith? What hobbies do you enjoy, what causes do you care about, what personal qualities do you pride yourself on (kindness, curiosity, humor)? These are the identity anchors that remain steady even if your business card changes. In truth, our identities are naturally multifaceted – each of us "contains multitudes," as the poet Walt Whitman said. We play many roles in life, and nurturing those varied roles can protect us from shattering when one role is lost. Research in psychology supports this: people with multiple sources of identity (e.g. family, hobbies, civic engagement) tend to be more resilient in the face of career upheaval, because they have other facets of themselves to draw strength from. For example, someone who, aside from being an engineer, also identifies as an avid hiker, a mentor to teens, and a father will have an easier time adjusting to retirement; he knows he's still *someone* – a hiker, a mentor, a dad – even without the engineering job. By contrast, someone who is *only* an engineer and nothing else may feel utterly lost if that job ends.

Redefining Identity and Purpose: Moving forward means consciously redefining your identity beyond your job. One helpful exercise, as suggested in a guide for retirees, is to actually think of new ways to describe yourself *instead* of your old title. Where you once might have said, "I'm a surgeon," you might reframe it as, "I'm someone who loves helping others heal." The first is a job; the second is a broader purpose that could be fulfilled through various outlets (teaching, volunteering, mentoring, etc.). In retirement coaching, they often encourage people to find new roles in the community: *"Where you were once an accountant, for example, you're now a mentor, volunteer, grandparent, student, memoirist, or artist."*. In other words, fill in the blank: *Now I am a _____.*

42

It could be something you used to enjoy but set aside, or something you've always wanted to explore. Setting new goals can also help reignite a sense of purpose. They need not be as grand as your past achievements; they just need to be meaningful to you. Maybe you always wanted to write a book, learn a language, restore an old car, or contribute to a cause in your community. Goals like these can *"energize you, provide a sense of purpose, and help to redefine your identity"* in this new chapter. You're not *losing* ambition or drive; you're redirecting it toward personal growth and fulfillment rather than external validation.

For those still in high-powered careers, it's not necessary to wait for a crisis to begin this process. The ideal is to cultivate a rich identity outside of work long before you ever leave. Recall the advice from the PhD who struggled after grad school: she later realized she needed to "learn who [she is] without academia" by grounding herself in "friends and hobbies outside of the university". In other words, don't let the university (or hospital, or office) be your whole world. If you diversify your life with relationships and activities unrelated to your title, the end of that title will not hit as hard – there will be other sources of joy and pride to catch you. A commenter on the physician's blog put it succinctly: *"Developing a healthy life outside of work is the best protection we have"* against losing ourselves. This might mean setting boundaries to ensure you spend time with family, or rekindling an old passion (music, gardening, sports) even during your career. These outside interests and connections act like lifeboats when the storm of career change comes.

From Breakdown to Breakthrough: People who have gone through the "vanishing self" crisis often emerge with powerful insights. They learn that *failure to separate self from title* was a recipe for pain, and they take steps to ensure it doesn't happen again. A former lawyer who now helps others transition away from law emphasizes that it's critical to remember *"your job is not your identity,"* and to actively *"discover who you are without basing it on what you do for work."* This might involve exploring dormant interests, spending more time with loved ones, or even seeking therapy or coaching to reinvent oneself. It certainly involves self-compassion – recognizing that you are worthy and whole even when you're not "achieving" in the eyes of the world. Some people make peace with the idea that their career was just one expression of their talents, and that they can repurpose those talents elsewhere. For instance, a retired surgeon might find a new calling in teaching anatomy to high schoolers, deriving satisfaction from sharing knowledge without the "M.D." title in active use. A former executive might channel their leadership skills into organizing a community initiative or mentoring young entrepreneurs. In doing so, they often realize the core of their identity – maybe a desire to lead, create, heal, or teach – never truly depended on the old job title; it was a quality within them that can manifest in new ways.

It's worth noting that "beyond the letters" doesn't mean you must abandon everything about your former role. It's about *integrating* that role into a broader self, not erasing it. You can honor the years you were a doctor or professor as an important part of your life story while also knowing you're more than that chapter. One academic who went through post-PhD turmoil later found comfort in the thought, *"I do and can exist beyond the university."* She remembered the curious, creative person she was even before the PhD, and realized those qualities still existed, ready to shape a new path. Likewise, an ex-lawyer might acknowledge, "Yes, I practiced law for 10 years, and I learned a lot from it, but I'm also a traveler, a mother, a volunteer, and a budding novelist." The letters after your name – M.D., Ph.D., Esq., CEO – are letters you earned, but they are not the sum total of *you.*

Moving Forward: Rebuilding identity is not an overnight process; it's a gradual journey of self-rediscovery. Practical steps can help. Some people find it useful to journal or talk with mentors and friends about their strengths and values outside work. Others engage in new activities to see what resonates – perhaps joining a class or club unrelated to their profession, which can both spark joy and introduce them to people who know them as *just themselves*, not as an impressive title. In the words of one physician blogger giving advice to colleagues: *"Love your job… But don't let it define you."* Enjoy the fulfillment your career brings, strive for excellence, but also root your sense of self in things that last – family, friendships, health, personal passions, and principles. Jobs may come and go (and institutions, as he wryly noted, *"won't always love us back"*), but those deeper aspects of self will endure.

Finally, remember that identity is an evolving story. It's okay if your answer to "Who am I?" shifts over time. In fact, it's healthy. Today you might be a professor; tomorrow you might reinvent as an entrepreneur or a mentor or an advocate for a cause – all while still being *you.* Embracing that flexibility is liberating. It means a setback or change in one role doesn't have to shatter your whole self-image. You can say, *"I am more than my title. I contain multitudes, and I can write new chapters for myself."* That mindset transforms the vanishing of one self into the emergence of another. When identity is no longer lost in a title, it can finally be found in a more authentic, resilient place – at the core of the person, where no title can ever fully define or confine you.

Chapter 4

Success Under Scrutiny – Redefining What "Making It" Means

The Mirage of Success

Society often paints a glittering mirage of what success looks like: high income, prestigious titles, luxury possessions, and public acclaim. From afar, these markers of "making it" shimmer with promise – but up close, many achievers find the oasis was an illusion all along. A growing body of research reveals that chasing wealth, status, and fame can leave people unexpectedly unfulfilled. In fact, a landmark study from the University of Rochester found that reaching materialistic or image-driven milestones *contributed* to worse well-being – those who achieved extrinsic goals like riches or beauty actually experienced more negative emotions (such as shame and anger) and more stress-related physical symptoms. This striking finding confirms what some who "have it all" quietly admit: the traditional trophies of success often fail to nourish the soul. The outward trappings may impress others, but internally the individual can feel empty or even *worse* than before.

It turns out that the promised land of conventional success isn't what it seems. The CEO with the corner office and seven-figure salary might also be battling anxiety or burnout. Surveys of high-level executives show alarming rates of stress and dissatisfaction despite their accomplishments.

One global study of over a thousand executives found 82% of senior leaders reported intense exhaustion symptomatic of burnout, and nearly all of those felt their mental health had declined as a result. In other words, climbing to the pinnacle of corporate success often brings crushing pressure and emotional strain, not lasting contentment. Even fame and fortune can prove to be a psychological dead end. Comedian Jim Carrey once quipped that he wishes everyone could get rich and famous and do everything they ever dreamed of, just to realize it's not the answer – a sobering insight echoed by scientific evidence and countless personal stories. We frequently see celebrities and top performers, seemingly living the dream, yet struggling with depression or a sense of hollowness. The mirage of success promises happiness "once we get there," but when we arrive, the expected bliss evaporates into the dry air of reality.

Why would achieving our society's highest goals leave us feeling unfulfilled or even miserable? Part of the paradox is adaptation: the human psyche quickly gets used to new gains, then hungers for more. Psychologists describe a "hedonic treadmill" effect, where after a high achievement, our happiness spike is brief and we soon revert to a baseline state. The fancy new car or big promotion gives a thrill at first, but within days or weeks that thrill fades into the background of life. Researchers Brickman and Campbell, who coined the hedonic treadmill concept, found that even major positive events bring only *ephemeral* boosts in happiness before our expectations rise and we're back to feeling "normal". In practical terms, the goalpost of "enough" keeps receding. The mirage retreats further into the distance the more we chase it. What's worse, chasing socially prized success can crowd out the truly fulfilling experiences. Time devoted to earning more money or admiration often crowds out opportunities for meaning and connection – like relaxing with loved ones or pursuing a passion – which are the real sources of lasting satisfaction. Ironically, the very pursuit of status and wealth can create a life starved of the deeper nourishment that makes life worthwhile. The result is a perplexing scene: from the outside, someone may look successful – the accolades, the lifestyle, the "trophies" are all there – yet inside they feel anxious, joyless, or disconnected. The first step in redefining success is recognizing this mirage for what it is: a false promise that external achievement alone will make us happy. As studies have now demonstrated, material success does not automatically translate to emotional fulfillment, and in many cases it can intensify stress and dissatisfaction despite the shiny veneer of accomplishment. Seeing through this illusion sets the stage for a more authentic understanding of what it means to "make it" in life.

External Validation Trap

One reason the traditional success formula often disappoints is that it's based on external validation – living by other people's definitions of achievement. From childhood onward, many of us are handed scripts for success written by well-meaning parents, teachers, or society at large: get the top grades, attend an elite school, land a high-paying job, win awards, and so on. These are *external* markers, and chasing them can become a psychological trap. High achievers frequently fall into a pattern of seeking approval and applause from others – bosses, peers, family – and in doing so, they may lose sight of what truly matters to them personally. The result is a hollow victory: achieving goals that look brilliant on paper but feel meaningless in one's heart. Narrative accounts abound of people who reach impressive heights only to realize they were climbing the wrong ladder – living someone else's dream, not their own. For example, consider the young attorney who became a lawyer to please her parents: she makes partner at a prestigious firm, yet finds herself inexplicably empty, wondering, "Whose life am I living?" Such stories illustrate the emptiness that comes from devoting years to goals that were never really *yours* to begin with. When our definition of success is borrowed from others, even our victories can ring false.

Psychologically, the external validation trap is pernicious. It conditions a person to measure their worth by other people's praise and expectations, rather than their own values or joy. Success becomes a performance, an ongoing quest to prove oneself worthy in the eyes of the audience – whether that audience is one's parents, social media followers, or an abstract "they" representing societal norms. This can box even high achievers into a narrow identity: you are only as good as your last accolade. Researchers and therapists have observed that many unfulfilled achievers internalized early on that they *had to achieve to be worthy of love and respect.* One psychotherapist describes how "the grownups in their lives [often] focused on childhood achievements" so much that these individuals absorbed the idea that they must continuously succeed to have value. In this mindset, achievements are not a source of joy or personal development – they are a *necessity* for validating one's very existence. The calculus is brutal: if I ever stop achieving, I stop being "good enough." This belief can drive people to incredible heights, but it also leaves them unable to ever rest or feel content. As one analysis put it, "Stop achieving, and you stop being lovable" – a distorted but powerful fear ingrained in the validation-seeker.

Living by others' definitions of success thus creates a constant pressure to perform and prove. Externally-driven achievers often describe feeling like frauds or feeling trapped by their own resume. They have to keep feeding the approval loop – higher salary, bigger house, another award – hoping each time they'll finally earn the validation they crave. But external approval is a moving target: please one set of expectations, and another appears. Furthermore, any affirmation they do get is fleeting. Psychologically, external validation is like a sugar rush – a quick high followed by a crash, leaving one craving the next dose. The person ends up on an endless treadmill of *"What will people think of me next?"* or *"How do I measure up now?"* This is exhausting and anxiety-provoking. Indeed, high achievers caught in this loop often experience anxiety and depression behind their polished façades. They might be outwardly successful and even admired, yet internally they feel like they're living for everyone except themselves. The stress of constantly needing to prove oneself can erode any pride in one's accomplishments – each win is immediately overshadowed by the question of what *more* must be done to maintain others' approval. And if the applause ever stops, or someone else outshines them, the externally-defined achiever is left with a fragile sense of self. It's a precarious way to live: as the Fast Company writer Josh Dodes observed, these "Unhappy Achievers" appear to have it all, but deep down they feel *miserable* and can't even understand why.

The why often lies in this fundamental mistake – building one's success on someone else's terms.

Breaking free from the external validation trap starts with recognizing that success is not one-size-fits-all. Society's scoreboard – whether it's the highest GPA, a fancy job title, or an envy-inducing social media feed – is a shallow measure of a life's worth. Yes, a high salary or a trophy can be gratifying, but only if they align with one's authentic aspirations. Otherwise, they become just heavy gold-plated shackles. In recent years, cultural commentators have pointed out how we live amid an "achievement culture" where *reductive measures of success* (like the best school, the biggest trophy, the most followers) are treated as ultimates, when in fact they often lead to distress. The more we live for those measures, the more boxed-in we feel. The good news is that many people who have fallen into this trap eventually hear an inner voice asking, "Is this all there is?" That question, uncomfortable as it can be, signals an awakening. It's the first step to redefining success on your own terms – a theme we will return to. First, however, we need to examine another facet of modern success dysfunction: the "never enough" syndrome that keeps even successful people perpetually unsatisfied.

Never-Enough Syndrome

Never-enough syndrome describes the perpetual cycle of achievement where each accomplishment only breeds the urge for the next one, in a ceaseless quest that never truly arrives at contentment. Picture a climber who summits a peak, only to immediately fixate on a taller mountain in the distance – that is the life of many high achievers.

You finally make partner at the firm or earn tenure at the university, milestones that you labored for years to reach. You expected to feel *victorious*, maybe even to relax and savor it. Instead, an unsettling question pops up: *"Now what? Is this it?"* The anticipated euphoria gives way to a strangely familiar restlessness. Rather than quenching the thirst for success, achieving the goal only seems to amplify it. The bar gets raised: if I did *that*, then I should be aiming even higher next time. This phenomenon has both psychological and neurochemical roots. Neuroscience has found that the brain's reward chemical, dopamine, is most active during the *pursuit* of a goal, not when we actually attain it. In other words, the chase thrills us more than the catch. Dopamine surges as we strive, driving us forward, but when the goal is in hand, the brain's "reward" quickly recedes. The victory can feel oddly anticlimactic – a brief high followed by a sense of emptiness or normalcy. This is why that promotion or award which felt incredible at first might leave you surprisingly flat after a short time. Biologically, our brains are wired to keep hunting for the next prize, a useful trait for survival perhaps, but a recipe for chronic dissatisfaction in a world of endless goals.

Psychologists have long observed this "always climbing, never arriving" pattern in achievers. The "hedonic treadmill" concept, mentioned earlier, perfectly encapsulates it: as people attain more success, their expectations and desires rise in tandem, so they *never truly feel ahead*. It's like walking on a treadmill where the faster you go, the faster the belt beneath you runs – you remain in the same emotional spot. One study noted that high achievers' initial satisfaction from a win is *fleeting*, and they soon revert to their prior emotional state, prompting them to seek the next win. Similarly, management thinkers have identified a pattern called "summit syndrome" among overachievers: these individuals are so driven by stimulation and the adrenaline of striving that when they do reach a hard-won summit, they quickly lose interest or feel deflated. The peak, rather than offering lasting fulfillment, becomes a plateau of boredom until they find a new mountain to climb. In effect, success becomes an addiction – not to any substance, but to achievement itself. Like any addiction, tolerance grows; smaller accomplishments no longer give a buzz, so one needs bigger and bigger goals to feel that same excitement. Over time, this can lead to a constant, gnawing sense that nothing is ever enough. No matter how much you do, there's always a higher level, another competitor to beat, another goalpost moved farther out.

The consequences of never-enough syndrome are profound. People who by objective standards are enormously successful often struggle with feelings of inadequacy or discontent because they *dwell on the gaps* rather than the gains. They may tally their unmet goals more than their achieved ones. In fact, as authors Dan Sullivan and Benjamin Hardy observed in their work with high performers, "many—if not most—high achievers remain unhappy... and their unhappiness grows deeper with each external accomplishment". This sounds paradoxical, but makes sense in light of adaptation and rising expectations. For example, research cited by those authors showed that CEOs are about twice as likely to suffer depression as the general public, and entrepreneurs (the paragons of ambition) face elevated rates of depression, substance abuse, and even suicide. These sobering statistics highlight that accumulating success does not immunize one from mental health struggles – in fact, it may exacerbate them. The "never enough" mindset keeps even the winners feeling like they're losing. They achieve a massive victory, yet "their mind quickly goes to the next unreached achievement", denying themselves the satisfaction of the victory they just earned. Life becomes a series of checkboxes ticked, without pause to savor any of it.

Modern culture can intensify this syndrome. In our hyper-connected age, social media and constant benchmarking create what one psychologist called a "hedonic hamster wheel". We are inundated with images of others' achievements, which continually raises the bar for what we think we should attain. Perhaps you felt proud of your new car until you saw friends online flaunting bigger luxury cars; or you were content with your promotion until LinkedIn announced that a college classmate became a VP at an even younger age. Exposure to others' highlight reels can make any achievement feel insufficient by comparison. It's an endless race, because there will *always* be someone seemingly doing better. As a result, the satisfaction from our own milestones is even more short-lived – the new achievement "falls flat after just a few days" when we're constantly reminded of greater ones out there. The goalposts don't just move internally due to our own ambition; they're also pushed by external comparisons and an achievement-obsessed culture. No wonder so many accomplished individuals secretly feel like they're running on a hamster wheel – exerting tremendous effort yet never feeling they've truly "arrived."

Recognizing the never-enough syndrome is a crucial wake-up call. It forces us to ask: *What am I chasing, and why?* If every time we achieve something we immediately dismiss it and hunger for more, perhaps we've lost sight of the purpose of our goals. The point of success shouldn't be to constantly invalidate past successes and raise the stakes to absurd heights. Yet that's what happens when achievement becomes a mere habit or compulsion, rather than a meaningful pursuit. Realizing that this pattern is at work can help break the spell. It's not that ambition or striving is bad – on the contrary, challenging oneself can be deeply fulfilling. The problem is when striving turns into a desperate chase for its own sake, divorced from any sense of *enough*. In the next section, we turn toward how to escape that hamster wheel and redefine success in a way that can actually satisfy the human spirit. It begins by shifting the metrics from more, more, more to very different measures of fulfillment.

Toward True Fulfillment

After scrutinizing the hollow side of conventional success, a natural question arises: *So what does genuine fulfillment look like?* How do we escape the mirage, climb off the treadmill, and step out of the external validation cage? The journey toward true fulfillment starts with redefining success on our own terms – choosing metrics of a good life that resonate with our innermost values and needs, rather than what society trumpets. This is not an overnight switch, but a gradual shift in perspective. It means pausing to ask ourselves tough but liberating questions: "What do I really want out of life, beyond the accolades? What brings me meaning and joy, even if no one else is watching or applauding? When do I feel most alive and content, and how can that be part of my definition of success?" In moving toward answers, research and real-world wisdom suggest that true fulfillment tends to come from intrinsic sources – things like personal growth, relationships, purpose, and well-being – rather than the extrinsic trophies we've been discussing. Studies have shown that individuals who focus on intrinsic aspirations (for example, becoming a better person, building loving relationships, contributing to community, or improving their health) report much higher satisfaction and well-being as they progress in those areas. They experience more positive emotions, richer social connections, and even fewer physical signs of stress compared to those chasing money, status, or image. In short, success feels *real* when it aligns with inner values and meets fundamental human needs, not just when it checks a societal box.

A conceptual reminder that we each face a choice: pursue a life of balance and meaning, or run ourselves into burnout chasing someone else's definition of success. True fulfillment often requires redefining what "winning" really means.

One of the most compelling findings in psychology is that connection and meaning trump wealth and fame in contributing to a good life. The Harvard Study of Adult Development, an extraordinary 80-year study tracking hundreds of lives, found that close relationships, more than money or fame, are what keep people happy over the long term. Those with supportive relationships and community fared better in health and life satisfaction, whereas high status or riches alone were not reliable predictors of happiness. This doesn't mean that one must renounce career success or material comfort; rather, it suggests that we should balance our "success portfolio" with the kinds of investments that truly pay emotional dividends. Think of things like time with family and friends, engagement in enjoyable activities, service to others, and personal passions – these often bring a sense of fulfillment that no award or salary could replace. True success might be better measured in moments of meaning and joy: the fulfillment of mentoring a younger colleague, the pride in creating something useful or beautiful, the joy of shared laughter with loved ones, or the peace of mind that comes from living in alignment with one's principles. These are not always quantifiable on a resume or LinkedIn profile, but they are central to a life well-lived.

To move toward genuine fulfillment, it's helpful to redefine what "making it" means for you personally. This could be a very individual definition. For one person, it might mean having a balanced life where work, family, and self-care are all honored – a success defined by balance rather than burnout. For another, it might mean doing work that is meaningful, even if it's not lucrative or famous – a success defined by purpose rather than public recognition. Some may define success as the ability to keep learning and growing, or to have the freedom to spend their time on what matters to them. There's no wrong answer except one: a definition of success that leaves you perpetually dissatisfied and disconnected from yourself. As Viktor Frankl, the great psychiatrist and Holocaust survivor, wisely noted, "Don't aim at success. The more you aim at it and make it a target, the more you are going to miss it. Success, like happiness, cannot be pursued; it must ensue…as the unintended side effect of one's personal dedication to a cause greater than oneself.". In other words, true success is a byproduct of pursuing what is meaningful to you. If you focus on what gives you meaning – whether it's helping others, expressing your creativity, raising a family, mastering a craft, or any endeavor that lights you up – then a sense of success *will naturally follow* as "unintended side-effect." This is a radical reframe: success is not a trophy to chase, but a state that ensues when you live according to your values and passions.

The closing of this chapter is not the end of the conversation but the beginning of a transformation in how we evaluate our lives. "Success Under Scrutiny" means we've interrogated the default assumptions about achievement and found many of them wanting. Now, armed with that insight, we can start to craft a more fulfilling vision of success. As we proceed into the following chapters, consider carrying these reflections with you. What if you let go of one "hoop" you've been jumping through that isn't truly yours? What might you gain in peace or self-respect if you did so? How might you redefine "making it" so that it includes not just *achieving*, but *being* – being happy, being connected, being true to yourself? The path toward true fulfillment invites us off the hamster wheel and onto a more personal, meaningful journey. This journey is about setting your own pace and direction, guided by internal values rather than external applause. It doesn't necessarily mean abandoning ambition; rather, it means aiming your ambition in a direction that actually fulfills you, not just impresses others. In the chapters ahead, we will explore practical ways to pursue this redefined success. For now, take heart in the hopeful truth that success is what you make it. By redefining its meaning to align with what genuinely fulfills you – balance, purpose, joy, or contribution – you can finally step off the treadmill and start truly arriving in your own life, every day. Each of us has the power to choose a more gratifying definition of "making it," and in doing so, to achieve a success that isn't just shiny on the outside, but deeply satisfying on the inside.

Chapter 5

From Burnout to Balance – Strategies for Sustainable Success

Burnout is Real – and You're Not Alone. In the intense world of high-pressure careers, success often comes at a personal cost. Physicians, attorneys, academics – all report staggering levels of burnout, the state of chronic exhaustion and disengagement from work. The World Health Organization now classifies burnout as an occupational "syndrome" resulting from workplace stress that hasn't been successfully managed. Classic symptoms include feeling utterly depleted, growing cynical or distant toward your job, and seeing your effectiveness plunge. In recent years, nearly half of U.S. doctors said they had at least one sign of burnout, and in one survey 77% of lawyers in a state Bar admitted to feeling burned out by their work. These numbers underscore that burnout isn't a rare weakness – it's a widespread challenge in modern professional life.

Why does this matter? Burnout isn't just feeling tired; it can derail careers and harm quality of work. Exhausted doctors are more prone to errors, and frazzled lawyers or professors can become less effective despite their long hours. In fact, as burnout worsens, job performance and even personal health can spiral downwards. Studies show burnout in physicians contributes to higher turnover (many doctors consider cutting back or leaving practice) and even lower patient satisfaction and safety. For lawyers, burnout has been linked to more mistakes and rising attrition as well. Clearly, sustainable success requires breaking the burnout cycle. The encouraging news? Burnout is *not* an inevitability of success – it is preventable and reversible with conscious changes. High-achievers around the world are finding ways to set boundaries, practice self-care, seek support, and realign their work-life priorities to thrive in demanding fields. In this chapter, we explore these strategies in depth. Grounded in both real-world stories and cutting-edge research, the sections that follow will show how you can climb to great heights in your career without sacrificing your health or happiness. Sustainable success is possible – and it starts by shifting from burnout to balance.

Setting Boundaries – Practical Tools for Carving Out a Healthier Life in High-Pressure Careers

One of the first steps from burnout toward balance is setting firm boundaries in your work life. For driven professionals, this can be challenging – you may feel compelled to say "yes" to every request, work every evening, and handle everything yourself. But the truth is that trying to "do it all" is a recipe for chronic overload. Learning when (and how) to say "no" is a powerful skill to protect both your well-being and your effectiveness. It might feel uncomfortable at first, but consider this: if you're working 60- or 70-hour weeks, are those extra hours really productive? Research indicates that beyond roughly 50 hours a week, productivity starts plummeting. In fact, one famous analysis by Stanford's John Pencavel showed that output becomes almost negligible after 55–

60 hours – fatigue and mistakes cancel out the extra work you attempt. In other words, when you chronically overwork, you actually accomplish less (and often need to fix more errors) than if you had rested once you hit a reasonable limit. Boundaries on work hours aren't just about sanity – they're about sustaining high performance.

Consider a narrative example: A senior surgeon at a major hospital was in the habit of staying late every single night, believing this dedication was necessary for patient care. But as exhaustion set in, she noticed more lapses in concentration and a creeping sense of cynicism about her job. Finally, after a near miss in the OR, she made a change: she spoke with her department chief and set a boundary to leave by 6:00 PM at least three nights a week – no exceptions unless there was a true emergency. At first she feared backlash, but something interesting happened. Her colleagues respected her clarity; some even admitted they too wanted better balance. More importantly, she found that with a defined end-of-day, she became *more focused and efficient* during work hours. Knowing she had to hand off tasks by 6 forced her to prioritize better. Within weeks, her fatigue eased and her effectiveness actually improved. Patients commented on her increased attentiveness, and she felt happier at work and at home. This story echoes many real experiences of professionals who set limits – when you carve out space for life and rest, your time at work tends to become more productive and creative.

Of course, boundary-setting isn't always straightforward in practice. Many fields have an "always on" culture, where late-night emails or weekend calls are the norm. Unclear expectations can trip up even those who *want* to set limits. As executive coach Nataly Kogan observes, the issue is that awareness of boundaries is not the same as implementation. A lawyer might *know* she shouldn't be available 24/7, but if her firm never explicitly discusses after-hours communication, she may feel guilty ignoring a Sunday email. Kogan gives a common example: a partner fires off emails on a Saturday; the associate thinks, *"I should set boundaries and not reply,"* but fears looking uncommitted if she waits until Monday. The root problem is lack of clarity – neither side has talked about it. The solution, Kogan suggests, is proactive communication: have a conversation on the team about what "off-hours" really means, and set *explicit, context-specific expectations.* Perhaps the rule becomes that weekend emails are answered Monday unless marked "urgent," or team members take turns being on-call. Such agreements remove the ambiguity that fuels guilt and stress. Boundaries work best when everyone understands them.

Beyond policies, setting boundaries requires personal resolve. It means recognizing that saying "no" at times is not a dereliction of duty – it's an investment in your long-term capacity to do good work. Consider the data on vacations: Lawyers who take their vacation time to unplug not only return with more energy, but are less likely to commit errors in their practice. Many law firms now actively *encourage* taking regular breaks for this very reason. Yet a culture of overwork can be hard to shake. A 2024 attorney survey found that the average lawyer took only 9 days off in a year – and even then, 73% of them still did work on at least half of those "off" days. Shockingly, a mere 3% managed to do no work at all on their vacation. This inability to disconnect is a classic sign of poor boundaries and contributes heavily to burnout. To change it, one must *choose* to disconnect. That might mean setting an auto-reply saying you'll respond next week, or literally turning off work phones in the evening.

It might feel like the sky will fall if you're not available. But as one attorney realized after finally guarding her Sunday as a no-work zone: *"Clients didn't fire me, the firm didn't collapse – instead I showed up Monday sharper and ready to solve problems."* In fact, numerous studies confirm that reasonable limits on work hours lead to better performance. Employees who get adequate rest, sleep, and personal time tend to be more engaged and make better decisions. By contrast, chronically overworked individuals experience stress-related declines in memory, mood, and even basic cognition when fatigue sets in. So if that voice in your head says "you should do it all," answer back with science: sometimes less is more. Setting boundaries – whether declining an extra case load, leaving the hospital at a set time, or simply *saying "no" to requests that exceed your bandwidth* – is not laziness or letting others down. It's preserving your capacity to excel at what *truly* matters. Give yourself permission to be a high achiever *and* a human being with limits. Paradoxically, once you do, you often achieve even more in the ways that count.

Mindfulness & Self-Care – Evidence-Based Techniques to Build Resilience into Your Routine

Preventing burnout isn't just about working less; it's also about replenishing yourself so you can handle stress better. That's where mindfulness and self-care routines come in. Far from being indulgent luxuries, habits that support your physical and mental health are essential – the foundation of resilience. Think of it this way: in high-pressure jobs you are like an elite athlete of the mind. Just as marathoners need rest days and good nutrition, knowledge workers and caregivers need recovery practices to perform at their peak. In this section, we explore proven techniques – from meditation to exercise – that strengthen you against stress. And these aren't fuzzy feel-good tips; they're backed by solid research showing real reductions in burnout symptoms.

One powerful tool is mindfulness meditation, the practice of training your attention to stay present. Mindfulness can be as simple as spending 5–10 minutes a day in quiet breathing or using a guided app to observe your thoughts without judgment. It might sound too simple to matter, but studies are increasingly demonstrating profound benefits. For example, a recent large study at The Ohio State University introduced an 8-week mindfulness program to hundreds of healthcare workers – nurses, doctors, staff – and the results were striking: participants' burnout levels dropped by 26% on average, with nurses seeing a 36% reduction in burnout after the course. Those who practiced mindfulness not only felt less exhausted, they also reported higher resilience and work engagement. As the lead researcher, Dr. Maryanna Klatt, noted, *"Mindfulness-based interventions can be used to build individual resilience, buffer the detrimental effects of occupational stress and enhance professional well-being."* In other words, mindfulness acts like a protective shield for your mind, helping you take life's punches without falling apart. Other studies in high-stress professions echo these findings. In the legal field, a study published in the *Journal of Occupational Health Psychology* found that lawyers who underwent mindfulness training had significantly lower emotional exhaustion and higher job satisfaction compared to those who didn't.

And research compiled by the American Bar Association shows mindful lawyers report better concentration and problem-solving abilities – a calmer mind can actually make you a sharper advocate. For professionals who thrive on cognitive performance, this is a game-changer: caring for your mental state *is part of* optimizing your productivity.

Real-world example: An overworked corporate attorney – let's call her Jane – reached a point where every day felt like sprinting through a minefield of stress. She started experiencing panic on Sunday nights and noticed her fuse at home was incredibly short. At a colleague's suggestion, Jane tried a beginners' yoga and meditation class at a local studio. Initially skeptical ("I'm not really the yoga type," she thought), she soon found that those morning sessions became a sanctuary. The combination of movement, deep breathing, and focused attention on the present moment did wonders for her anxiety. After a month, Jane made it a daily habit – a 20-minute gentle yoga and mindfulness routine every morning before checking her email. The effect was apparent not only to her (she felt more balanced and less reactive) but even to her coworkers. One day in a contentious meeting, a partner remarked, *"You seem very composed under pressure – what's your secret?"* She realized that her mindfulness practice was enabling her to step back, take a breath, and respond deliberately rather than just react. It was helping her "respond" rather than "react," a key aspect of resilience. In her own words: "Opposing counsel still gets under my skin sometimes, but now I catch myself, breathe, and approach things more calmly" – a shift that ultimately benefits her clients and team as well.

Mindfulness is just one aspect of self-care. Equally important are physical health habits: regular exercise, adequate sleep, and good nutrition. These might sound obvious, but busy professionals often neglect them, viewing self-care as secondary to productivity. In truth, they are deeply intertwined. Exercise, for example, has well-documented effects on mood and stress hormones – even moderate aerobic exercise a few times a week can lower your cortisol (the stress hormone) and boost endorphins, those natural mood elevators. Healthy eating and staying hydrated stabilize your energy levels and concentration throughout the day. And sleep – perhaps the most undervalued necessity in high-achieving circles – is critical for cognitive function, emotional regulation, and even for preventing burnout. Studies have consistently found that chronic sleep deprivation contributes to burnout by impairing your ability to cope with work demands. On the flip side, prioritizing sleep (7–9 hours for most adults) can markedly improve your focus and patience at work. One survey of lawyers recommended prioritizing sufficient sleep and regular breaks as key strategies to prevent fatigue and burnout – not exactly rocket science, but advice often ignored.

Consider another personal story, this time of a medical professor and researcher. He was juggling grant applications, patient care, and mentoring students – a workload that routinely bled into nights and weekends. His physical health deteriorated; he'd put on weight and felt perpetually drained. At one point, a minor health scare forced him to re-evaluate his lifestyle. With some mentorship from a colleague, he made a commitment to self-care non-negotiables: three mornings a week he'd go for a 30-minute run, and he'd actually *take* his lunch break to eat a proper meal (instead of scarfing down junk at his desk). He also started using a meditation app for 10 minutes in the afternoon when stress peaked. The changes were small but steady. Over several months, he lost the extra weight and noticed that his afternoon slumps disappeared – he had more energy for that late-day meeting or for reviewing a student's thesis. Psychologically, he felt more in control and less like a victim of his schedule. Research supports these anecdotes: even simple deep-breathing exercises at work have been shown to increase calm and reduce stress markers. The key is consistency – integrating these practices into your *routine* so that caring for your mind and body becomes as habitual as checking your email.

It's worth emphasizing that self-care is not selfish; it is essential. High performers sometimes fall into the trap of thinking, "I don't have time for a break or a workout; too many people are counting on me." If that's your mindset, flip it around: because so many people count on you, you owe it to them (and yourself) to maintain your well-being. Otherwise, you'll eventually crash – and be of no help to anyone. Treat self-care as part of your job. Block it on your calendar like you would a meeting. Maybe you have a 15-minute mid-morning "meeting" with yourself to stretch, walk around the building, or do a quick breathing meditation. These micro-practices can significantly reduce acute stress. For instance, a Stanford study found that just 5 minutes a day of simple breathing exercises led to lower anxiety and improved mood over a month. When done regularly, these small resets prevent stress from snowballing throughout your day.

Lastly, don't overlook mental health support as a form of self-care. Engaging in therapy or counseling is not a sign of inability to cope – it's a proactive strategy to build coping skills. Many professionals, from attorneys to academics, quietly see therapists or coaches to navigate the intense pressure of their fields. An attorney who starts therapy may learn cognitive techniques to manage anxious thoughts before a big trial. A PhD student might work with a counselor to develop strategies for imposter syndrome or procrastination that's adding to burnout. These supports can be transformative. Think of therapy or coaching as personal training for your mental fitness. In a later section we'll talk more about seeking help, but it bears noting here: self-care sometimes means knowing when to reach out for professional help to bolster your resilience.

In summary, making self-care and mindfulness part of your routine builds a kind of *emotional armor*. It doesn't mean you won't face stress – you will, especially in high-stakes careers – but it means stress won't penetrate as deeply or linger as long. You'll recover faster from setbacks and maintain your passion for your work. Just as importantly, you'll enrich your life *beyond* work. Because sustainable success isn't just about what you achieve in your career, but also about enjoying a healthy, fulfilling life outside of it. Mindfulness and self-care help you show up as your best self in all spheres of life. And if guilt or doubt ever creeps in – remember the evidence and stories above. Taking care of yourself is one of the smartest, most responsible investments you can make in your professional journey.

Finding Support – The Power of Camaraderie, Mentorship, and Asking for Help

High achievers are often accustomed to being the one others rely on – the doctor reassuring patients, the professor guiding students, the lawyer advising clients. With that responsibility, many develop a false belief that they must "tough it out" alone and always appear strong and self-sufficient. However, one of the most effective antidotes to burnout is recognizing that you are not alone and actively seeking support from peers, mentors, or professionals. Burnout feeds on isolation. When you think you're the only one struggling, you're less likely to speak up or seek help, which only deepens the cycle. Breaking that cycle involves a bit of courage to reach out – but the payoff in reduced stress and renewed motivation is enormous. Let's explore how finding support can lighten your emotional load and provide practical solutions, through both research and real-world examples.

First, consider the role of peer support groups or communities. Many professions have begun to organize forums where colleagues can openly share their experiences and coping strategies. In medicine, for instance, the concept of the "Balint group" or other physician support meetings has gained traction – doctors coming together to discuss the emotional aspects of patient care in a confidential setting. These groups validate that it's normal to feel grief after a patient's death or frustration with systemic issues, and they help practitioners process those feelings in a healthy way. A recent Kaiser Permanente initiative called the Peer Outreach Support Team (POST) provides one-on-one peer support to physicians after tough clinical events. The feedback was overwhelmingly positive: doctors who engaged in the peer support program reported feeling "less isolated, less frustrated, and less victimized" by stressful events, and saw improved morale in their departments. Simply knowing that a colleague understands exactly what you're going through – because they've been through it too – can be a huge relief. One physician described the peer support as an environment where she could share her thoughts and feelings with no judgment and no repercussions, which made her feel "less alone in my situation". That sense of shared understanding is powerful. It reminds us that struggle in high-pressure jobs is common, not a personal failing, and that by sharing we can collectively find solutions (or at least sympathy and advice).

Support can also come in the form of mentorship. Having a more experienced professional to confide in and seek guidance from can significantly buffer the stress of career challenges. Mentors can offer perspective – they've weathered similar storms and can reassure you that rough patches are temporary or navigable. For example, a junior professor feeling overwhelmed by tenure demands might find solace after talking to a senior faculty mentor who recalls, *"Yes, I remember that phase – here's what helped me…."* In one illustrative story from a law firm, a young associate was grappling with self-doubt and perfectionism. She mustered the courage to tell a senior partner, "I'm intimidated and I feel like I can't do good work because I'm so anxious about making mistakes." To her surprise, the partner – a highly respected attorney – opened up about his own past struggles as a junior: the long hours, the fear of failure, even bouts of burnout he'd faced. This candid conversation was a turning point. The associate realized that what she was experiencing was *normal* and that even successful people have hard times. It also gave her practical tips, as the mentor shared how he coped and learned to overcome those hurdles. *"One way to overcome these obstacles is to be willing to share and talk about it,"* the partner told her, emphasizing that talking about difficulties is not a sign of weakness but a strategy for growth. This kind of mentorship dynamic can transform a toxic "suffer alone" culture into one of openness and mutual support. The truth is, most organizations want to retain their talent; good leaders would rather know you're struggling and help you, than silently watch you burn out and quit. By seeking mentorship or peer counsel, you give them the chance to support you – and you give yourself the chance to learn from their experience.

In addition to informal peer connections, structured professional support like coaching or counseling can be immensely beneficial. Many companies and institutions now offer Employee Assistance Programs (EAPs) with counseling services, or even professional coaching for burnout and work-life balance. A noteworthy study at UCLA in 2025 found that offering small-group coaching sessions to physicians led to nearly a 30% reduction in burnout rates among participants. These sessions allowed doctors to discuss challenges in a guided setting and develop coping strategies together. Interestingly, the small-group format was even more cost-effective and, in this case, more impactful than one-on-one coaching. This underlines a crucial insight: there is "power in numbers." When people come together, even in a facilitated group, to support each other, the results can outperform solo solutions. Similarly, some law firms have started peer-coaching circles for associates, and universities have group workshops for faculty on managing stress. If your workplace offers something like this, consider joining – it might feel odd at first to discuss personal struggles in a group, but many find it cathartic and encouraging.

And let's not forget the value of therapy or counseling outside of work. Speaking confidentially with a psychologist or counselor can help you process work stress, build better boundaries, and address any deeper issues like anxiety or depression that often accompany burnout. For example, a professor we'll call Maria reached a point where she dreaded going to campus – she felt like a fraud (classic imposter syndrome) and was near tears nightly grading stacks of papers. At her university's recommendation, she started seeing a counselor. In those sessions, Maria learned techniques to challenge her negative thoughts ("I'm not doing enough"; "I'm a failure") and was gently pushed to prioritize self-compassion. Over time, therapy helped her regain confidence and set small boundaries, like not answering student emails after 9 PM. It also simply gave her a *safe space* to vent about academic politics and workload without fear of judgment. The improvement in her outlook was noticeable to colleagues; she began to smile and collaborate more, once the weight of isolation was lifted. The lesson: Professional help is not a last resort – it can be a preventive step that equips you with emotional tools to thrive. Just as you wouldn't hesitate to consult a specialist for a physical ailment, don't hesitate to consult one for mental well-being. Many highly successful doctors and lawyers quietly have therapists or coaches on speed dial, and that's one reason they remain successful and sane!

Finally, creating a culture of support often means being willing to show *your* vulnerability to others, which can encourage them to do the same. If you're a leader or even a mid-level professional, consider that you can set an example. When appropriate, share a bit about your own challenges and how you addressed them – it humanizes you and signals to others that it's okay to speak up. For instance, a hospital department chair noticed residents and junior doctors were suffering in silence. In a meeting, he opened up about a time early in his career when he almost quit due to burnout, and he described how a peer group and mentor pulled him through. This simple act led one resident to approach him later and admit she was in trouble emotionally – which meant they could connect her with help and adjust her schedule before things got worse. Support often starts with *someone* breaking the ice.

In summary, seeking and offering support is a strength, not a weakness. Humans are social creatures; we're wired to thrive in community. The myth of the solitary hero who handles everything alone is just that – a myth. In reality, even the brightest experts benefit from a sounding board, a shoulder to lean on, or advice from someone who's walked the path before. By reaching out – whether to a colleague, a mentor, a support group, or a professional – you lighten the load you carry and gain insight that can help you cope. You also might discover new strategies to manage work that you hadn't thought of, drawn from others' experiences. And simply knowing *"I'm not the only one"* provides emotional relief that can prevent that downward spiral of burnout. So next time you're tempted to just grit your teeth and bear it, remember that sometimes the bravest thing you can do is raise your hand and say,

"I could use some help." You might be amazed at how many people are willing to extend it – and how much difference it can make in your journey from burnout to balance.

Work-Life Realignment – Restoring Balance by Realigning Priorities at Work *and* Beyond

The final piece of the burnout-to-balance puzzle is a broader realignment of how work fits into your life. This goes beyond day-to-day tweaks and asks a bigger question: Are your priorities and expectations set up to support a sustainable, fulfilling life? Achieving balance often requires both personal shifts (in mindset and habits) and, when possible, adjustments in your work environment. This section offers pragmatic tips on delegating, renegotiating workloads or flexibility, and letting go of perfectionism in favor of a focus on what truly matters. The empowering message here is that sustainable success is *not* about squeezing work into every crevice of life, but about making conscious choices so that your life outside of work is valued as much as your life at work. In fact, when organizations adopt healthier work cultures – reasonable hours, respect for downtime, and support for employees' personal lives – they often see *better* results, not worse. Balance can boost performance, not hinder it.

Let's start with personal realignment of priorities. Many driven individuals fall into the trap of perfectionism and all-or-nothing thinking. You might hold yourself to impossibly high standards in *every* aspect of work – every email must be thorough, every project flawless, every client utterly satisfied. While high standards can drive excellence, perfectionism in excess becomes a straight path to burnout. Psychiatrists who study burnout note that perfectionist traits – being extremely dutiful, never saying no to more work, and refusing to take breaks – put people at high risk of burning out. As one expert put it, *"They work long hours. If they're told to take a break, they say, 'No, I've got more work to do.' All of that is fine—until it's not."* Eventually, the perfectionist mindset leads to exhaustion and diminishing returns. If you recognize this in yourself, it's time to challenge the belief that everything rests on your shoulders or that anything less than 110% is failure. Realignment might mean re-defining what "success" looks like in a given task. Not every email needs a dissertation; not every committee meeting needs you to volunteer as chair. Identify the truly critical areas where your extra effort yields benefit (for example, double-checking a contract for errors is worth it; spending an extra hour tweaking the font on a report is not). In less critical tasks, give yourself permission to do a "good enough" job and move on. Prioritize the big rocks – the things that align with your core professional goals or values – and let the smaller pebbles go. This shift can be surprisingly liberating. Many professionals discover that when they stop micromanaging themselves on trivial details, they free up energy for creative thinking and big-picture work that is ultimately more satisfying and impactful.

Hand-in-hand with easing perfectionism is the skill of delegating and negotiating workload. If you're in a leadership role or any position where you can distribute tasks, delegating is crucial. High achievers often think "It'll be faster if I do it myself" or doubt others' ability to handle the task. But taking on everything is a fast track to burnout and also deprives colleagues of growth opportunities. By delegating tasks that others can do, you lighten your own load and empower your team. A physician leader might delegate some administrative duties to a practice manager, or a professor might let a teaching assistant handle routine grading and only review the highlights. A common worry is quality control, but you can often mitigate that by setting clear expectations and checking in at key milestones rather than doing it all personally. Delegation is not dumping work on others – it's *sharing* work in a way that benefits everyone. Remind yourself: your time is a finite resource and should be used where you add the most unique value.

If you're not in a position to delegate, consider negotiating for more flexibility or resources. For example, many professionals have successfully negotiated alternative working arrangements that better suit their life, such as one day a week working from home, a slightly reduced schedule, or shifting hours earlier or later to accommodate family time. If you have proven your value to an organization, you may have more leverage than you think to request adjustments. The key is to frame it not as an "escape from work" but as a way to be *more effective*. Perhaps you tell your firm, "I'd like to experiment with working from home on Fridays to have a quieter environment to focus on deep work – I believe this will improve my output on complex tasks." Many employers are increasingly open to flexibility, especially after seeing productivity maintained (or even improved) during remote work experiments. In fact, global trials of a four-day workweek (where employees worked 80% of the time for 100% pay) found that employee stress, burnout, and fatigue all declined significantly, while productivity *improved* or stayed the same. Such results are reframing how management views work-life balance – not as coddling employees, but as smart strategy to keep people engaged and performing well. You might not get a four-day week, but even a modest change like having one less clinic day, or shifting some duties to a deputy, can make a big difference. Be prepared to present a plan: for instance, if you propose a job-share or hiring an assistant, explain how it would work and how it ultimately benefits the organization (fewer mistakes, better client service, etc.). The worst they can say is no – but they might say yes, or at least open a dialogue about workload that leads to improvements.

Another aspect of realignment is advocating for systemic changes in your workplace culture. This could range from pushing for reasonable caps on hours, to starting a discussion on email norms (e.g., no expectation to reply after hours), to encouraging leadership to invest in wellness resources. It might feel beyond your scope, but remember that many positive changes start with grassroots efforts. A group of residents at one hospital spoke up about the need for a mental health debrief after traumatic cases – hospital leadership implemented a peer support debrief system as a result. In a law firm, associates formed a committee to address burnout which led to the firm hiring an outside consultant to recommend better workflow and break policies. If you and your peers are struggling, consider banding together to propose solutions. Organizations are slowly waking up to the reality that burnout costs them – in turnover, absenteeism, and lost productivity. (Physician burnout, for instance, is estimated to cost the U.S. healthcare system $4.6 billion a year due to doctor turnover and reduced clinical hours.) So, making the work culture healthier isn't just nice for employees, it's financially smart for employers. Use that fact if you need to bolster your case. Cite examples of forward-thinking organizations: *"Company X introduced meeting-free Wednesday afternoons and saw a boost in project completion rates,"* or *"Y University created a flexible summer schedule and reduced faculty turnover by 30%."* There is a growing body of evidence that healthier work practices lead to more sustainable success.

Now, let's bring it back to the individual level with a short empowering story. Picture an accomplished but frazzled lawyer – call him Alex – who, after 10 years of 60-hour weeks, realized he hardly knew his kids and his health was suffering. One day, Alex decided to realign his priorities. He still loved law, but he also valued being a present father and staying healthy. So, he made a bold ask: he negotiated with his firm to go to a *reduced-hour schedule, 80% of full-time,* and in exchange he'd take a slight pay cut and focus on mentoring junior lawyers (a role he enjoyed). To his surprise, the firm agreed – they didn't want to lose a talented attorney and respected his honesty. In his new arrangement, Alex left the office by 5 PM most days. He spent evenings coaching his daughter's soccer team and got back into running. What happened at work? Far from sliding into obscurity, Alex became an even better lawyer. With more energy and a clearer head, his efficiency skyrocketed. He delegated more to juniors (now that he had time to coach them), which grew their skills and eased his burden. He started coming up with creative legal strategies during his morning runs. Clients noticed his improved focus and remained very satisfied. And crucially, Alex was *happier.* He'd found a balance that worked for him, and it showed in both his work output and personal life.

Not everyone can make such a dramatic change, but the principle stands: align your work with your life values whenever possible. If family, hobbies, community, or health are important to you (and they are for most of us), they should have a place in your schedule and not just the leftovers after work devours the week. Schedule that painting class on Thursday night, or block off a weekend for a short trip, or commit to volunteering on Saturday mornings – whatever brings you joy or fulfillment outside of work. These aren't "extras"; they are part of the fabric of a well-rounded, satisfying life. When you pursue interests and relationships beyond your job title, you also create a buffer against work stress. A setback at work feels less catastrophic when your whole identity isn't only "doctor" or "lawyer" but also "gardener, parent, friend, hiker, musician," etc. Your self-worth and happiness have multiple pillars.

Realigning priorities may also involve reassessing what success means to you personally. In academia or professional fields, it's easy to get caught in external metrics: the next promotion, the prestigious award, the salary raise. There's nothing wrong with ambition, but make sure the ladder you're climbing is leaning against a wall you truly care about. Sometimes people burn out chasing goals that, deep down, aren't aligned with their genuine values. A PhD student might realize they actually find industry work more fulfilling than an academic tenure-track (and that's okay!). A physician might choose a lower-paying specialty with better hours because it allows time to volunteer or pursue other passions. These choices can be tough – they require honesty with oneself – but aligning career choices with personal values is key to long-term happiness.

Sustainable success does not have to follow one narrow definition. It's about thriving in *your own* definition of a good life.

In workplaces that encourage work-life integration, the benefits become evident. Employees are more engaged, creative, and loyal. As mentioned earlier, experiments like the four-day workweek show that when people are well-rested and have time for life, they often perform better and show up more fully at work. Even on a smaller scale, a company that discourages late-night emails or a department that rotates on-call duties fairly will have staff who feel respected and therefore are more motivated. If you're in a leadership position, you have the power to champion these cultural shifts. If not, you can still influence by example – set boundaries, use your vacation time, and share how it helps you. Sometimes seeing one respected colleague take a real lunch break or actually unplug on vacation gives others permission to do the same.

Pragmatic tip: One strategy some organizations use is the idea of *"strategic renewal"* – encouraging short breaks during work (a walk around the block, a 5-minute stretch) and regular vacations or sabbaticals. This is not wasted time; it's time that fuels high-quality work. As an individual, practice strategic renewal in your day: after 90 minutes of intense focus, take 10 minutes to recharge (grab a coffee, chat with a friend, do a quick breathing exercise). This aligns with our ultradian rhythm (natural cycles of energy) and can prevent the slow drain of working non-stop. On a larger scale, plan annual or semiannual realignments: maybe every six months you sit down and evaluate your balance. Are you working too many weekends? Have you dropped hobbies you used to love? Use that check-in to adjust – perhaps schedule a catch-up with friends or book that family vacation you've postponed.

Ultimately, realigning work and life is an ongoing process, not a one-time fix. Life phases change (early career vs mid-career vs late career, parenting young kids vs empty nest, etc.), and your needs for balance will change too. The key is to remain mindful of the balance equation and not let work automatically dominate by default. Keep steering your ship intentionally rather than letting the currents of workplace culture carry you away. Advocate for yourself and for a healthier workplace when you can. And remember, valuing your life outside of work isn't a detriment to success – it's a prerequisite for *sustainable* success. People who cultivate rich, balanced lives bring their best selves to work *and* to their families and communities. They avoid the flame-out and instead have the fuel to keep achieving, year after year, with satisfaction.

As we conclude this chapter, take heart in the pragmatic and empowering truth it offers: Burnout is not a badge of honor, and balance is not a sign of slacking – it's the strategy of long-term champions. By setting boundaries, practicing self-care, seeking support, and realigning priorities, you can excel in your demanding career *and* lead a fulfilling life beyond it. The journey from burnout to balance is highly personal, but you now have a toolkit of evidence-based strategies and inspiring examples to guide you. The professionals who have implemented these changes – the doctors reclaiming their weekends, the attorneys finding solace in meditation, the professors leaning on peers, the entrepreneurs redesigning their work-life fit – show us that it can be done. They rediscovered joy and purpose in their work and life once they made these shifts. Sustainable success is about more than surviving your career; it's about *thriving* in all aspects of who you are. With courage to change and commitment to these principles, you too can move from the brink of burnout to a place of balance, where success is truly sustainable and happiness is part of the journey, not just a distant destination.

Chapter 6

Reclaiming Identity – Rediscovering the Person Behind the Professional

Professional success can sometimes come at the cost of personal identity. Many high-achievers wake up one day to realize that the person they are outside the office has faded into the background. Consider the story shared by a psychologist about a high-powered attorney named "Dan," who one morning found himself curled up on his bathroom floor, unable to face the day. He had poured everything into his career until his job title became his whole identity – and when the pressures mounted, he felt he had nothing of himself left to stand on. Sadly, Dan's experience is not unique. Surveys show that over 55% of Americans derive their sense of identity from their job title, a precarious foundation given that careers can change in an instant. If who you are is completely tied to being "Dr. So-and-so" or "Partner at Firm X," what happens if that title is lost or no longer fulfilling? The good news is that it's possible – at any stage of life – to step back and rediscover the person behind the professional. This chapter will guide you through that process in a grounded and inspiring way, showing how to reconnect with passions, build relationships beyond work, realign with your core values, and ultimately reclaim your own narrative. The aim is to help you remember that your worth far exceeds any business card and to provide practical strategies to anchor your identity in what truly matters to you.

Reconnect with Passions

One of the first steps to reclaiming your identity is to revive the hobbies and interests that once lit you up, before your climb to success swept them aside. Picture a dedicated physician in her forties dusting off the violin she used to play in college. During years of medical training and 80-hour workweeks, that violin lay silent in its case. But now, as she draws the bow across the strings in her living room after work, she rediscovers a part of herself that existed long before she was called "Doctor." In a poignant real-life example, one doctor admitted that he had neglected his beloved hobbies during medical school and residency, only to return to gardening, traveling, and reading during a period of burnout – and found that these personal passions "helped pull [him] out of the depths of burnout" and allowed him to lead a more fulfilling life even as he continued practicing medicine. It turns out that rekindling such interests is not just a nostalgic indulgence; it can be life-saving for your sense of self.

Modern science strongly supports the healing power of hobbies. Engaging in activities purely for joy and personal meaning has measurable benefits for mental health and even physical well-being. For instance, creative hobbies can literally lower your stress hormones: in one study, 75% of participants saw a decrease in cortisol (the stress hormone) after just 45 minutes of making art, and it didn't matter whether they had any prior artistic skill. This means you don't have to be a concert pianist or skilled painter – simply the act of creating or doing something you love is enough to reduce stress. Another study from New Zealand found that on days when people spent time on creative pastimes, they felt significantly happier and more energized – with a higher sense of "flourishing" – the next day. The positive mood boost from painting a picture, writing in a journal, or cooking a new recipe can spill over, giving lasting effects beyond the activity itself.

Reigniting old passions also helps you reconnect with your authentic self, the "you" that might have been set aside for your career. Psychologists note that hobbies are more than just distractions – they actually enrich your identity by adding new facets to how you see yourself. If you start drawing again regularly, you might gradually come to see yourself as an "artist" and not only a scientist or lawyer. As one physician reflected, *"developing hobbies is a way of developing and becoming yourself."* He pointed out that if you doodle once you probably wouldn't call yourself an artist, but if you draw regularly, your self-image can change – "maybe 'artist' becomes an identity that fits". In other words, pursuing passions helps you grow into a more complete version of you. This expansion of identity is profoundly healthy. It ensures that your self-worth isn't confined to one narrow role dictated by your job.

Importantly, hobbies can replenish emotional energy rather than drain it. Professional burnout is often a sign that all of one's energy is going into work with nothing restoring it. Hobbies serve as a vital counterbalance. There's even evidence from the medical field: physicians who maintain active hobbies have significantly lower levels of burnout and feel more connected to their work on the whole. The same likely holds for lawyers, professors, or anyone in high-pressure careers. By spending a few hours a week doing something for the pure love of it – whether it's strumming that guitar, tending a garden, or hiking a trail – you refill your own cup. You return to work not as "just a cog in the machine," but as a more grounded, creative, and energized person, which paradoxically can make you better at your job and certainly happier in life. In fact, many high achievers credit their hobbies as keys to their success, not hindrances. One startup founder who took up horseback riding in the midst of a stressful business venture said it made her feel "like an unstoppable force" in all aspects of life. Even Olympic gold medalist Tom Daley has cited his quirky hobby of knitting as a source of focus and calm that helped him perform under pressure. When you reconnect with a passion, you tap into a well of joy and confidence that can spill into everything you do.

Reconnecting with passions can also mean rediscovering simple joys like spending time in nature or moving your body for fun rather than duty. Perhaps you once loved cycling or taking long walks in the woods, but now you barely see daylight outside of your commute. Try carving out time for that weekend bike ride or a morning in the park – even a short 10-minute dose of nature can markedly improve your mood, focus, and overall well-being. If you used to play on a sports team or sing in a choir, consider joining a local league or community chorus now. These outlets not only give pleasure; they remind you that you're a multifaceted human with talents and interests beyond the office. Over time, the goal is to feel the spark of enthusiasm in your eyes again – the same spark you might remember from youth, when you lost track of time sketching, playing pickup basketball, or tinkering with a beloved project. Those passions are still part of you, and reigniting them will help you reclaim the "you" that might have been overshadowed by the professional title. As you do, you'll likely notice stress melting away and a sense of balance returning. One study of older adults across 16 countries found that people with hobbies reported higher overall life satisfaction, better health, and fewer depressive symptoms compared to those without hobbies. The researchers noted that hobbies engage us in creativity, self-expression, and relaxation, and often involve social connection – all ingredients of good mental health. In short, dusting off those old joys isn't frivolous; it's a proven way to reconnect with your authentic self and boost your happiness in a lasting way.

People and Places Beyond Work

Another crucial step in rediscovering the person behind the professional is to cultivate roles, relationships, and communities that have nothing to do with your job title. It's time to be "more than just Dr. So-and-so" in the eyes of others – and, importantly, in your own eyes. If your social circle and activities currently all revolve around your field, you're missing out on a whole spectrum of identity that exists beyond work. Advisors often urge graduate students and young professionals to nurture friends and hobbies outside of work for this very reason: your value and well-being shouldn't be 100% tied to the lab, the firm, or the hospital. When you engage with people who don't care about your resume, you get to show up as fully yourself, not as a walking business card.

Real-life narratives illustrate how liberating and enriching this can be. One scientist-in-training recounts how she started a casual crafting club during grad school – just a few peers getting together to crochet and chat as a break from research. That little hobby group ended up not only helping them cope with the stresses of graduate life, but also built a supportive community and even led to outreach projects (like crocheting a giant 3-foot monarch caterpillar to raise science awareness!). In interviews, she found that those "out-of-lab" experiences and friendships made her stand out as a well-rounded person. More importantly, the club reminded everyone involved that they were more than just researchers chained to their desks. They became teammates, friends, and creators together. Similarly, imagine an accomplished surgeon who joins a weekend soccer league where none of the other players are in medicine – to them, she's not "Dr. Smith," she's the reliable goalkeeper or the enthusiastic teammate who brings oranges for the team at halftime. In those moments, she gets to be valued for her personality and camaraderie, not her CV. Such experiences can be profoundly validating. They prove that your worth isn't confined to your professional skills; you have so much more to offer and to enjoy.

Building relationships beyond work provides an emotional safety net and a broader base for your self-esteem. No matter how passionate you are about your career, work will have ups and downs. Who do you turn to on the rough days? Research on graduate students – who are often in a work-absorbed phase of life – has noted that having an emotional support system is vital to survive the "bumpy ride" of challenges. The same applies in mid-career: a spouse, friends, or community members who care about you (the person) can celebrate your good days and see you through the bad days. When a deal falls through or you have a terrible week at work, a close friend with whom you share a common hobby or a sibling who just loves you as *you* can remind you that your life is so much bigger than that setback. Psychologically, it's healthier to distribute your "identity eggs" in many baskets. As one writer put it, it's important to have diverse sources of self-worth besides work – and friends and family can be among the greatest of those sources. Strong relationships can bolster your self-image and confidence regardless of how things are going in the office. For example, you might be going through a slump in publishing research papers or in hitting sales targets, but if you have a loving bond with your kids, a softball team that counts on you, or a faith group or community charity where you volunteer, you still get to feel *needed, appreciated, and competent* in other roles. Those feelings act as a buffer; your entire self-esteem doesn't plummet with one work disappointment.

There is also a special benefit to friendships and communities completely outside your professional bubble. They offer fresh perspectives and a sense of reality beyond your work world. One PhD student wrote about how enriching it was to make friends *outside* his department and even outside academia altogether – they gave him "a refreshing change of pace and a glimpse of what life beyond grad school was like". Crucially, these friends could support him when he was struggling with work, precisely because they had some distance from it. They weren't in the weeds of the same problems, so they could offer unbiased advice and a listening ear without also being stressed by that exact issue. He also noted a practical point: when he vented about his work frustrations to these outside friends, he didn't feel guilty that he was burdening them – whereas venting to a lab mate who was under the same stress might feel like adding to their load. This highlights an important truth: friends who know you as more than a co-worker can often be there for you in ways colleagues cannot. They see *you*, not your title. They can provide solace or solutions that are not colored by the workplace environment. Moreover, these "outsider" friends often introduce you to new activities and viewpoints that enrich your identity. Through them, you might discover a love of a new cuisine, an interest in local politics, or simply the reminder that there are whole worlds out there where your job title doesn't matter in the slightest.

Cultivating a life beyond work does take effort, especially for busy professionals, but it's richly rewarding. It might start with something as simple as scheduling regular dinners with family, or joining a local club (a book club, a hiking group, a religious congregation – anywhere you'll meet people with shared interests apart from work). If you've moved for your career and feel isolated, consider platforms like community classes or Meetup groups to find people in your city who gather around everything from photography to volunteering. It's true that making new friends as an adult can be daunting – one reason experts advise not to neglect social life when you're younger is that it does get harder to meet like-minded people later, when routines get entrenched and social circles shrink. But it's far from impossible. You may be surprised how warmly the world welcomes you when you step outside your professional silo.

Neighbors, fellow parents at your children's school, fellow gym enthusiasts – connections are everywhere.

Keep in mind, too, that relationships beyond work often prove that you have a value no performance review can measure. Perhaps you volunteer at a community kitchen on Sundays and the patrons know you as the kind soul who always has a smile and an encouraging word. To them, you're a helper and a friend, not an accountant or an engineer. That experience can be deeply affirming. In fact, volunteering and community involvement not only make you feel good spiritually, they also correlate with tangible boosts in mental health. A U.K. study in 2020 found that people who volunteered regularly were more satisfied with their lives and rated their overall health as better, with those volunteering at least a month reporting better mental health than non-volunteers. Serving others can reduce stress and increase happiness; volunteers often describe a sense of pride and identity in their role helping others, which raises self-esteem. By being known as, say, "the coach of the kids' soccer team" or "a Big Brother/Big Sister mentor" or "an activist in the neighborhood," you expand your identity in beautiful ways. You become someone who is valued for your humanity and heart, not your business card. And the paradox is that this makes you stronger and more resilient back in your career. When the company or institution you work for sees that you maintain a rich life outside its walls, you subtly remind *yourself* (and them) that you are not just a title – you are a whole person. That realization is incredibly empowering.

Your Values as North Star

Amid the noise of career demands and external expectations, your core personal values are like the North Star – a constant point of reference that can guide you back to who you truly are. Refocusing on what *really* matters to you, independent of your job status, is a powerful way to anchor your identity. To begin, take a moment to reflect: *What values do I hold most dear?* Perhaps it's integrity, creativity, justice, compassion, freedom, or growth. These guiding principles often get us into our professions in the first place – a young person may pursue medicine out of compassion or science out of curiosity – but years of routine can make anyone lose sight of these original motivations. Rediscovering and living by your values will illuminate parts of your identity that no job title can ever fully capture.

Let's look at a couple of narrative examples. Imagine a successful corporate lawyer, whom we'll call *Alex*. Alex went into law because he deeply values justice and wanted to use his skills to help the vulnerable. Fast forward 15 years, and he's now a partner at a firm mainly defending big companies in lawsuits. The pay and prestige are great, but he feels an ache, a sense that something is missing. In his limited free time, Alex decides to volunteer one evening a week at a legal aid clinic for low-income clients – drafting wills, helping with tenant rights cases. At first, it's just pro bono work. But soon he realizes those few hours reignite a passion he had forgotten. By acting on his core value of justice in a context outside his job, Alex reconnects with the idealistic, motivated person he used to be. He comes alive helping people who sincerely need an advocate. That fulfillment starts spilling over into his day job; he even finds new meaning there by mentoring junior attorneys about why the law matters. In another scenario, consider *Priya*, a physician-researcher who values lifelong learning and curiosity. Her job is highly specialized, and after a decade she feels stagnation creeping in. So Priya starts taking an Italian language class in the evenings – entirely unrelated to medicine, simply because she loves Italian culture and the challenge of learning. It's humbling and exhilarating to be a beginner again. She travels to Italy for a vacation and can chat with locals now. This experience lights up Priya's identity in a way her narrowly focused career hadn't in years. She is not "just a doctor" – she's also a linguist, a student of the world, a traveler. By honoring her value of learning, she becomes more fully herself, which in turn brings fresh energy into all parts of her life.

These stories underscore a key lesson: living in alignment with your values gives you a sense of self no professional status can provide. Psychology research supports this truth. When you clarify and prioritize your personal values, you gain a stronger sense of purpose and authenticity in life. Acting according to your values – rather than just reacting to external pressures – makes you feel that *you* are in charge of your life's direction, leading to greater self-respect and confidence. In fact, engaging in activities that reflect your core values has been shown to improve mental well-being and even alleviate feelings of depression and anxiety. For example, if one of your cherished values is compassion, you might volunteer at a hospice or simply spend more quality time caring for a relative or neighbor in need. Such value-driven actions can be profoundly rewarding; as one article noted, psychologists believe that reconnecting with important personal values can serve as a strong motivator for recovering mental wellness. It helps pull you out of ruts by reminding you *why* life is worth living in the first place.

To use your values as a North Star, start by articulating them clearly. You could journal about moments in your life when you felt truly proud or fulfilled – what values were you honoring in those moments? Was it honesty, adventure, kindness, or something else? Once you've identified a handful of core values, ask yourself: *Am I living these values day-to-day, or have they taken a backseat?* If, say, creativity is a top value, yet your daily routine has little room for creative expression, that's a sign to integrate a creative practice into your life. It could be as simple as baking inventive desserts on weekends, or as significant as seeking a more innovative role at work. If family or community is a core value, are you investing enough time in those connections? Realigning life with values might involve tough choices (perhaps cutting back hours to spend time with family, or switching to a role that better matches your ethical standards), but those choices pay off in a deep sense of integrity and self-esteem. Remember, your values form a significant part of your personal identity – they "shape you into your authentic self and give you a sense of purpose". When your actions resonate with what you truly care about, you feel "like your truest self", and that is a powerful foundation that remains steady even if your external circumstances shift.

Living by your values also tends to attract the right people and opportunities into your life. You'll find that when you communicate and act in line with your principles, you connect more authentically with others. You may even discover new communities who share those values, further reinforcing that you are more than your job – you are the sum of what you believe in and stand for. For instance, someone who values exploration and adventure might join an outdoor trekking club and suddenly have a whole new circle of friends who know them as the avid hiker with a great sense of humor – not as an overworked executive. Another who values faith or service might get involved in a faith-based group or charity where their contributions are measured in dedication and kindness, not in professional accolades. These experiences can be affirming: as the National Alliance on Mental Illness notes, dedicating time to a cause you care about can give you a renewed sense of purpose and direction when you feel lost, and even provide a "sense of pride and identity" from the role you play in that sphere. In short, your core values are a compass pointing to the real you. By following that compass, you ensure that your identity isn't at the mercy of a job or degree; it's rooted in what truly matters to you, which is far more enduring.

Writing Your Own Narrative

The final section of reclaiming your identity involves something deeply personal and empowering: writing your own narrative. Up until now, you've looked at external facets – hobbies, people, values – that help reclaim who you are beyond work. The capstone is to integrate all of your experiences, professional and personal, into a cohesive story that you author. Instead of seeing yourself as just the sum of degrees, job titles, and roles assigned to you by others, you can reframe your life story in a way that honors *all* of you – the struggles overcome, the lessons learned, and the whole, evolving person you've become. This process is a gentle but powerful way to heal any identity wounds that may have accumulated over years of feeling "not enough" or overly defined by one aspect of life. By actively defining who you are in your own words, you regain control of your narrative and set the stage for a future where you write the next chapters, not your job or anyone else.

One practical and proven tool for this is journaling – the simple act of writing down your thoughts and life events. It might surprise you how effective this can be. Psychologist James Pennebaker, a pioneer in the field of expressive writing, found in his research that when people write about significant life experiences or upheavals, they often experience remarkable improvements in their health and well-being. "When people are given the opportunity to write about emotional upheavals," Pennebaker notes, "they often experience improved health. They go to the doctor less. … If they are first-year college students, their grades tend to go up." The very act of forming a narrative on paper or screen helps your mind process and make sense of events. When something painful or defining happens – say, a career setback or a personal loss – our thoughts can swirl in a loop. Writing translates those experiences into language, creating a story that you can reflect on. In doing so, it's as if you take a mental jumble and give it structure. You produce, as one article put it, "a physical piece to contemplate," allowing you to better grasp what's going on and perhaps approach your situation more objectively. There's a kind of magic in seeing your own life in narrative form: it turns nebulous emotions into concrete words, which you can evaluate, question, and re-interpret. Studies suggest that building a narrative around life events helps shift them into long-term memory in a more organized way, instead of leaving them as raw, unprocessed feelings. In essence, you become the storyteller, not just the passive character, of your life.

To make this practical, you don't have to be a skilled writer or spend hours every day journaling. Even occasional reflective writing can be therapeutic. Pennebaker's method often asks people to write freely for just 15–20 minutes a day over a few days about something deeply important or impactful, with no concern for grammar or polish – just raw honesty. Many who do this report feeling better, sleeping better, and having a clearer outlook afterwards. If writing isn't your preferred mode, you can achieve similar reflective processing through speaking – for example, seeing a counselor or even recording voice memos for yourself describing pivotal moments in your life and what they meant to you. The key is to start connecting the dots in your story: How did you get here? What have you overcome? What values guided you, even unknowingly? What patterns do you notice? By asking these questions, you begin to see continuity and meaning rather than a series of unrelated events or just a resume timeline.

Narrative techniques are used in many forms of therapy because they help people reshape their identities in healthier ways. In narrative therapy, a concept known as "re-authoring" invites individuals to identify the dominant story they've been telling themselves ("I'm only worthwhile when I achieve X," or "I sacrificed everything for my career") and then rewrite that story to be more holistic and empowering. You might realize, for instance, that a challenge you once viewed as a failure was actually the seed of later growth – a plot twist that taught you resilience or redirected you to a path that aligned better with your values. By framing it that way in your narrative, the "failure" becomes a proud part of your personal legend, not an ugly stain. Likewise, you can give voice to parts of yourself that were quiet in the old narrative. Maybe your previous story was all about you as the diligent worker, but now you write in chapters about you the parent, the traveler, the friend, the musician. This expanded narrative validates all aspects of who you are. It also prepares you for the future. When you have a firm grasp of your life story – when you know *"this is who I am, these are the themes of my journey"* – you become much less fearful of change. Losing a job or retiring or starting something completely new doesn't shatter your identity; it simply begins a new chapter in the story of a person who is much more than any one role.

Some people find it helpful to actually write an autobiography or personal mission statement for themselves as a way of solidifying this. It could be a private document where you narrate your life from a first-person perspective, highlighting not the professional milestones, but the human milestones: times you acted according to your values, times you learned from mistakes, moments of connection and courage. Include those degrees and jobs, sure, but as *part* of the story, not the whole story. As you write, you might notice threads that weave through it all – perhaps a thread of curiosity driving both your career and your hobbies, or a thread of compassion in both your family life and work life. Identifying these threads can give you a sense of coherence: you start to see that you have always been "you," just expressing it in different arenas. And if there are painful parts of your story that still feel unresolved, writing them out or talking them through with a therapist can help you process and find closure, so that those chapters no longer define you, but rather inform you.

Importantly, you do not have to dwell on negatives constantly to benefit from narrative building. In fact, Pennebaker cautions that one shouldn't feel obligated to journal about traumatic events every day indefinitely – "standing back every now and then and evaluating where you are in life is really important", he says. The goal is reflection and understanding, not rumination. So you might set aside time periodically – perhaps once a week or when you feel particularly at a crossroads – to write about where you've been and where you're going. You can use prompts such as: *"What do I want my life to stand for?"*, *"How would I describe myself in a letter to someone who doesn't know me, beyond my job?"*, or *"What chapter might be the title of this current phase of my life, and what do I hope the next chapter will be?"* These kinds of prompts encourage you to define yourself in your own terms, reinforcing that you are the author of your identity, not just the role that society has cast you in.

By consciously authoring your own narrative, you also become more solution-focused about any identity-related pain. For instance, if you feel a sense of loss over time wasted or opportunities missed (a common midlife sentiment), you can reframe that in your story as *"I spent years climbing the corporate ladder because I believed hard work was the right thing – now I see that experience gave me skills and empathy, and I'm using it as a springboard to a more balanced life."* Suddenly, even regrets can be turned into lessons and motivation for positive change. In your personal narrative, you can be the hero who overcomes challenges, rather than a victim of circumstance. This doesn't mean ignoring genuine hardships – quite the opposite. It means honoring them as integral to the hero's journey that is your life. The result is a sense of wholeness: you start to appreciate how *all* of your experiences, in and out of work, have shaped the person behind the professional.

As you conclude this inner work, take a step back and read the story you're telling about yourself. Does it acknowledge all your roles – not just the worker, but perhaps the parent, friend, artist, adventurer, caregiver, learner – and all your values? If not, you have the power to edit and expand it. This ongoing process of narrative crafting is incredibly empowering. It ensures that no single chapter (like a career chapter) defines your entire book. You regain the starring role in your own life, rather than feeling like a minor character defined by a job or expectations. And looking forward, you can approach the future with excitement: you get to ask, *"What will the next chapter of my story be?"* Perhaps it's one where you integrate work and life more harmoniously, or one where you finally pursue a calling that aligns with your true self. With passions reignited, a supportive community around you, a clear set of values guiding you, and your personal narrative in hand, you can move into that future not limited by any one role. You are free to grow, change, and continue becoming the multifaceted, authentic person you were always meant to be. In claiming your own narrative, you reclaim *yourself*.

Chapter 7

Success, Redefined – Crafting a Fulfilling Future on Your Terms

Success on Your Terms

What does success truly mean to *you*? In a world full of trophies, titles, and external expectations, it's easy to default to society's checklist of achievement. Yet the reality is that success is entirely subjective – a unique, highly individualized journey shaped by our own values and experiences. One person's vision of success might be raising a healthy family or building a community clinic, while another's could be traveling the world or inventing a life-changing technology. The key is recognizing that your definition may never perfectly align with anyone else's. This is empowering: it means you have permission to break free from the mold and choose metrics of success that resonate with your *own* well-being and purpose.

Consider the most common regret people voice at life's end: *"I wish I'd had the courage to live a life true to myself, not the life others expected of me.".* This poignant insight, shared by a palliative care nurse who spent years listening to the dying, reveals how damaging it can be to chase someone else's idea of success. Many accomplished individuals—doctors, lawyers, professors—find that after decades of grinding toward society's next accolade, something still feels missing. Perhaps an elite surgeon realizes that amassing publications or a big house didn't bring the fulfillment they expected, or a lawyer senses that making partner at a prestigious firm, while a proud moment, isn't a cure-all for happiness. The lesson is clear: your life must be driven by *your* values. If you measure success only by external standards (salary, status, the letters after your name), you risk climbing a ladder propped against the wrong wall. As one university career panel concluded, *"success is entirely subjective… shaped by personal experiences, values, and a broader perspective beyond traditional measures or societal expectations.".* In other words, the sooner you define success for yourself, the sooner you can channel your energy into pursuits that genuinely resonate with you, rather than chasing illusions.

Defining success on your own terms starts with introspection. Take a step back from the noise of expectations and reflect: *What truly matters to me?* Maybe it's maintaining impeccable ethical standards in your medical practice, even if it means turning down a more lucrative job. Maybe it's prioritizing creative freedom in your research over the pressure to publish quantity over quality. When you connect with your authentic self – clarifying the core values and passions that drive you – you create a personal vision of success that is both motivating and sustaining. Indeed, aligning our careers with our inner values often yields a deep sense of purpose and satisfaction. Psychologists note that people who live according to their own values tend to feel a greater sense of meaning in life and less internal conflict, because they are not constantly at odds with themselves. In practical terms, this might mean a physician choosing a humble community health role because it aligns with her passion for service, rather than pursuing a prestigious department chair position that doesn't excite her. Or it might mean an academic turning down an administrative post in favor of working closely with students, because mentoring is what brings joy. There is no right or wrong answer – success can be as unique as your definition of a good life. The critical move is to claim the right to define it. By doing so, you set the stage for a career and life that feel *authentic* and deeply rewarding, rather than checking off someone else's list.

Intrinsic Rewards

Too often, high achievers find themselves chasing external validation – the award, the promotion, the social prestige – only to discover that these victories, while sweet in the moment, don't necessarily translate to lasting fulfillment. Modern psychological research offers a compelling explanation: intrinsic rewards, the inner satisfactions that come from meaningful pursuits, have a far greater impact on our happiness and well-being than extrinsic rewards like money or status. In fact, decades of studies within self-determination theory have shown that when people focus on goals that are inherently fulfilling – such as personal growth, close relationships, or contributing to their community – they experience greater life satisfaction, more positive emotions, and overall happiness. Conversely, chasing goals primarily for external approval or material gain has been linked to *lower* well-being and even higher anxiety and depression. As researchers succinctly put it, "all goals are not created equal" – a reminder that why we strive is just as important as what we strive for.

For example, imagine two physicians with equally illustrious credentials. One might devote extra hours to networking and boosting their public profile – an externally driven approach. The other focuses on building stronger relationships with patients and mentoring junior doctors – an intrinsically motivated path. Over time, the second doctor is likely to feel more nourished by their career. In one qualitative study of physicians who *loved* their work, a common theme was the joy derived from patient connections and making a visible impact on others' lives. These physicians cited moments like comforting a worried family, seeing a patient recover, or knowing their work filled an unmet need in the community as "extremely rewarding", giving them a profound sense of purpose. Their happiness wasn't coming from a higher paycheck or an award plaque on the wall – it was coming from the meaningful human experiences built into their day-to-day practice.

Likewise, consider a university professor who has achieved tenure and could coast on her research accolades. She discovers, however, that her true fulfillment comes from the intrinsic rewards of teaching and mentoring. Guiding a struggling student to find their confidence, or sparking a young researcher's curiosity in the lab, gives a rush of satisfaction that no amount of external praise can match. Psychologically, this makes sense: prioritizing intrinsic goals like learning, personal excellence, friendship, or community contribution feeds our basic human needs for growth, connection, and competence. Studies show that people driven by these internal goals report higher well-being and happiness than those fixated on extrinsic aims. In one long-running Harvard study, it was close personal relationships – not wealth, fame, or social rank – that emerged as the strongest predictor of a happy and healthy life. In fact, the researchers concluded that *"close relationships, more than money or fame, are what keep people happy throughout their lives".* Think about that: all the status in the world can't compensate for a lack of meaningful human connection or personal growth.

For high-achieving professionals, this is a call to shift focus. By all means, celebrate your diplomas and aim high in your field – but don't overlook the quiet, personal victories that truly sustain you. A doctor might find greater joy in a grateful smile from a healed patient than in a bonus check. A lawyer might derive deeper purpose from pro bono work that transforms lives than from winning yet another corporate case. A business leader might feel more pride when employees thrive under her mentorship than when quarterly profits edge up. By attending to these intrinsic rewards, you cultivate a career nourished by internal fulfillment. Over time, those inner rewards create a reservoir of motivation that external accolades simply can't provide. They remind you *why* you started on this path in the first place – and they keep that flame of passion burning bright when external applause dies down.

Balanced Ambition

Ambition has long been the driving force propelling professionals to excel. As a doctor, lawyer, scholar, or executive, you likely didn't get where you are without a healthy dose of it. But there's an important distinction between healthy, balanced ambition and the kind of single-minded drive that exacts a personal toll. The challenge is learning how to *continue striving for excellence without sacrificing yourself.* Can you aim high while still keeping your feet on the ground? The resounding answer: yes – if you consciously pursue balanced ambition that values well-being as much as achievement.

In practice, balanced ambition means setting inspiring goals *and* setting boundaries. It means working hard for your patients, clients, or projects, but not at the expense of your health, family, or inner peace. There is mounting evidence that maintaining a work-life harmony isn't just a feel-good slogan – it's integral to long-term success. Research finds that a positive work-life balance significantly boosts overall well-being, job satisfaction, and even productivity, whereas poor balance is strongly linked to stress, burnout, and health problems. In other words, burning the candle at both ends eventually burns *you* out, diminishing the quality of your work and life. By contrast, when professionals feel balanced and happy, they tend to be more productive, take fewer sick days, and stay creative and engaged in their careers. Excellence, it turns out, is fully compatible with (and may even depend on) rest, recreation, and relationships.

Real-world examples increasingly bear this out. Take the story of a high-powered attorney who, after years of 80-hour weeks at a prestigious firm, made a bold change: he moved to a smaller practice with saner hours so he could be present for dinner with his family. Colleagues were stunned – wasn't he torpedoing his chance at partnership? But a few years on, he found himself not only happier but actually more effective in his work. With a clearer mind and a fuller heart, he brought fresh energy to his cases during the day, and left the office with enough emotional reserve to enjoy evenings coaching his son's soccer team. He learned firsthand what research confirms: many people who chronically overwork come to deeply regret the life moments missed. In fact, one survey of older adults found a common regret was *"I wish I hadn't worked so hard,"* especially among men who felt they lost out on family time by being perpetually on the job. This regret suggests that success at any cost may not feel like success at all if it estranges you from loved ones or leads you to neglect your own well-being.

Academia provides another instructive tale. An accomplished scientist recalled how early in her career, she only celebrated the big wins – the major grant awarded, the paper in a top journal – and downplayed everything else. Minor successes were immediately followed by *"What's next?"* and she routinely sacrificed weekends and hobbies to chase the next breakthrough. She achieved a great deal, but also teetered on the edge of burnout, her passion eroding under constant pressure. It wasn't until a mentor advised her to start celebrating small wins and set humane limits that she rediscovered joy in her work. She began to take pride in incremental progress: a productive discussion with her lab team, a student's improved results, even the days she left the office early enough to join a yoga class. By redefining ambition to include *self-care and personal life*, she actually sustained her career with more creativity and longevity. Her publication record didn't suffer – if anything, her rejuvenated mental state led to more insightful research. This underscores a powerful message: it's possible to aim high while keeping your feet on the ground. In medicine, law, business, or any field, the highest performers are often those who pair drive with balance – who sprint when necessary, but also know when to jog or even rest.

Importantly, balanced ambition isn't about lowering your standards or becoming complacent. It's about *sustainable* striving. Think of it as running a marathon instead of a series of desperate sprints. You still cover the miles, but you pace yourself to avoid collapse. By doing so, you not only reach the finish line of your goals, but you're also in good shape to enjoy what comes after. Remember that success and well-being can coexist – and in the long run, each fuels the other. When you take care of your health and relationships, you're fortifying the very foundation on which career achievements are built. And when you achieve milestones in a state of balance, you actually get to savor them, rather than feeling too exhausted or empty to appreciate your own success.

Legacy and Purpose

As you advance through your career and check off milestones, it's natural for the question of legacy to start looming larger. Beyond the next accolade or promotion, what is the bigger picture of your life's work? What do you want to stand for, ultimately, when all is said and done? In this final section, we invite you to lift your gaze to the long horizon and consider how focusing on meaning and purpose can redefine success as a lifelong journey of contribution and growth, rather than a destination or a line on your CV.

Begin with a simple yet profound reflection: *How do I want to make others' lives better?* For many in healing and helping professions, this is the north star that led them into the field, though it's easy to lose sight of amid day-to-day demands. Re-centering on your personal mission can be tremendously energizing. Perhaps your mission as a physician is not just to treat diseases, but to empower patients with knowledge and compassion so they lead healthier lives. A lawyer's mission might be to advance justice, ensuring even the vulnerable have a voice. A scientist's mission could be to expand human knowledge in a way that helps society, and an educator's mission to shape minds and uplift the next generation. Defining this mission in clear, personal terms transforms success from a checklist into a meaningful narrative – *your* narrative. You move from simply amassing accomplishments to building a legacy that you can be proud of.

Thinking about legacy naturally shifts perspective from short-term wins to long-term impact. Instead of just asking "What's my next goal?", also ask, *"What do I hope will endure because of my work? What positive ripple effects do I want to set in motion?"* By focusing on such questions, achievers often find a renewed sense of motivation and fulfillment. Research in psychology supports this emphasis on purpose: having a clear sense of purpose in life is associated not only with greater life satisfaction but even with better health and longevity. In a study following over 6,000 adults for 14 years, those who reported a strong life purpose had significantly lower risk of mortality than those who felt aimless. The benefit of purpose was evident across all ages, from young adults to the elderly. In other words, orienting your life toward a broader meaning – something beyond just your own advancement – can literally help you live longer, healthier, and happier. That's a powerful incentive to look beyond the next accolade and invest in what truly matters to you.

Leaving a legacy doesn't necessarily mean doing something world-famous or monumental. Often, it is the cumulative impact of small, meaningful acts and initiatives that add up over a lifetime. A medical professor who mentors scores of young doctors, instilling in them not just clinical skills but also compassion, will see her legacy live on in each of their careers. A business leader who champions ethical practices and nurtures a positive company culture leaves an imprint on hundreds of employees and their families. A community lawyer who spends extra time educating clients and improving local policy might not make headlines, but over years she shifts the justice landscape in her town. These contributions are immeasurable in worth. They define success as *significance* – the knowledge that your being here made things better for others in some tangible way. Indeed, many leaders come to realize that moving from *success to significance* is the ultimate fulfillment: it's the difference between just adding accolades to your name and actually making a difference in the world.

Psychologists refer to this drive to contribute beyond oneself as generativity, a concern for establishing and guiding the next generation. Embracing generativity can markedly increase one's sense of accomplishment and well-being. In the workplace, studies have found that people who engage in mentoring and guiding others often experience *renewed* motivation, higher job satisfaction, and personal growth. Mentors frequently report that in helping others succeed, they themselves feel more fulfilled and purposeful. In fact, effective mentoring and legacy-building efforts create a virtuous cycle: they give you a sense of "greater life satisfaction, a sense of purpose, and lasting positive change" in your own life while also benefiting others. This is success redefined as a win-win – enriching others' lives even as you enrich your own inner life.

As we conclude this chapter – and this book – take a moment to envision the story of *your* success as it might be told in years or decades hence. What do you want the chapters to say? Perhaps it's the story of a physician who treated thousands with skill and heart, and also mentored future healers. Or a lawyer who could have chased only prestige, but instead chose cases that upheld her ideals and improved her community. Or a Ph.D. who used her knowledge not just to earn accolades, but to solve real problems and open doors for those after her. These are success stories that resonate because they are driven by meaning. They remind us that beyond the letters after your name lies a richer definition of success – one that *you* actively shape through the life you lead and the legacy you leave.

In redefining success on your terms, prioritizing intrinsic rewards, maintaining balanced ambition, and orienting your life toward legacy and purpose, you are crafting a future that is genuinely fulfilling. Such success is not a finish line but a journey – one where each step, each day of growth or contribution, is itself part of the reward. As you continue on that journey, remember that you hold the pen. You get to write the definition of a good life for yourself, and you can choose a definition that leaves you not only successful in the eyes of others, but deeply satisfied in your own heart. That is success, redefined.

Epilogue

The letters after your name will always be there—carved in diplomas, printed on business cards, whispered in introductions. But they no longer define the boundaries of who you are becoming.

You have walked through the valley of achievement's shadow, where accolades echo hollow and prestigious titles feel like beautiful cages. You have felt the weight of others' expectations pressing against your chest, making each breath a conscious effort. You have stared into the mirror of societal success and seen a stranger looking back.

And then you began the real work.

The tools in these pages are not mere concepts—they are bridges you have built between the person you thought you had to be and the person you are choosing to become. Each boundary you have set, each value you have reclaimed, each moment you have chosen presence over productivity has been an act of quiet revolution.

Your worth was never contingent on the next promotion, the next publication, or the next case won. Your identity runs deeper than any credential, flowing from sources that cannot be printed on résumés or measured in billable hours. You are not your achievements, nor are you diminished by them.

The path forward requires no additional degrees. No committee will vote on your worthiness. No external authority will grant you permission to live authentically.

You already possess everything needed for this next chapter: the wisdom to recognize your patterns, the courage to disrupt them, and the compassion to treat yourself as you would a dear friend. The emptiness that once felt like an ending was actually a clearing—space for something more genuine to take root.

Your real work begins now, and the harvest will be measured not in letters, but in the richness of a life reclaimed.

www.ingramcontent.com/pod-product-compliance
Lightning Source LLC
Chambersburg PA
CBHW070125030426
42335CB00016B/2265